Harvey Hook shares from his own experiences, as well as those of others, as he leads and instructs readers in developing their lives as difference makers. There is something in this book for everyone seeking to influence and inspire others. ZIG ZIGLAR
author and motivational teacher

If a burned and naked nine-year-old Vietnamese girl could turn the tide of an entire war, then imagine what you can do with your life. The truths revealed in *The Power of an Ordinary Life* will change you and your world forever. KIM PHUC
Victim of a U.S. napalm bomb
attack during the Vietnam War

Harvey Hook doesn't just write about making a difference, he does it! Using examples from Ashley Smith to Elisabeth Elliot to my daughter, Rachel Scott, Harvey challenges us to change the world. Sometimes it's the simple acts of kindness in obedience to God that revolutionize people's lives. I urge you to accept Harvey's challenge in *The Power of an Ordinary Life.* DARRELL SCOTT
founder, The Columbine Redemption

The most powerful preservation of history is captured not in events but through the lives of the people that lived it. *The Power of an Ordinary Life* will become a classic of our generation and future generations as it serves to capture the lives of those who made some degree of history in their time. I recommend this book for information, inspiration, and transformation. It's a winner. DR. MYLES E. MUNROE
founder, Bahamas Faith Ministries International

You have been called to a life of redemptive action. *The Power of an Ordinary Life* shows you how to create reconciling relationships in a lost world that will restore your friends to God and to the world he created.
DR. TONY EVANS
senior pastor, Oak Cliff Bible Fellowship

We need more people who understand the idea that one person empowered by God can change the world. *The Power of an Ordinary Life* takes that thought from wishful thinking to living reality. Why would any of us want to settle for less?   JOSH D. MCDOWELL
author and speaker

Whether you've survived the killing fields of Rwanda or enjoyed the abundance of comforts in America, *The Power of an Ordinary Life* offers indispensable insights for whatever path of life you are on.

IMMACULÉE ILIBAGIZA
Rwanda holocaust survivor, author of Left To Tell

God is the one who puts the power in an ordinary life. The moment we allow the Lord to live in us, we can meet any challenge. This book is a wonderful guide and companion as we pursue our true calling from God.   H. WAYNE HUIZENGA, JR.
president, Huizenga Holdings, Inc.

The easiest way for us to change the world is to first touch the person next to us. *The Power of an Ordinary Life* is the perfect blueprint for changing the world forever.   JACK HANNA
host, Jack Hanna's Animal Adventures

Time changes, world order changes, people change, nations change, and ethics change, but God never changes. The old excuse of "everybody else is doing it" will not hold up when we stand before God. In *The Power of an Ordinary Life,* Harvey Hook powerfully applies God's Word to today's events.   BOBBY BOWDEN
head football coach, Florida State University

the Power of an Ordinary Life

the
POWER
of an
ORDINARY LIFE

Discover the Extraordinary
Possibilities Within

HARVEY HOOK

TYNDALE HOUSE PUBLISHERS, INC. CAROL STREAM, ILLINOIS

Visit Tyndale's exciting Web site at www.tyndale.com

TYNDALE and Tyndale's quill logo are registered trademarks of Tyndale House Publishers, Inc.

The Power of an Ordinary Life: Discover the Extraordinary Possibilities Within

Designed by Jessie McGrath

Library of Congress Cataloging-in-Publication Data

Hook, Harvey (Harvey A.)
    The power of an ordinary life : discover the extraordinary possibilities within / Harvey Hook.
        p. cm.
    Includes bibliographical references.
    ISBN-13: 978-1-4143-1344-3 (hc)
    ISBN-10: 1-4143-1344-6 (hc)
    1. Christian life. I. Title.
    BV4501.3.H675 2007
    248.4—dc22   2007017405

Printed in the United States of America

13   12   11   10   09   08   07
 7   6   5   4   3   2   1

This book is dedicated to my parents:
Gilbert Charles Hook
7/22/1908 — 3/11/1982
and
Helen Gertrude (Beam) Hook
10/17/1914 — 11/25/1992
in memory of their simple faith and their simple ways
and to
the three beautiful women given to me by God:
my wife, Rita, and our daughters, Rebecca and Rachel,
for all they have taught me about life, love and living in the moment.

CONTENTS

CONTENTS

Acknowledgments

Every agent and publisher who rejected my manuscript: Thank you. You made me dig deeper, refine my thoughts, sharpen my pencil, and pursue the message that has now been published.

Jay Kesler and George Verwer: Thank you for opening the door to Tyndale House Publishers.

Mark Taylor: Thank you for taking my call.

Ken Petersen: Thank you for believing in my message when no one else would.

Linda Schlafer and Dave Lindstedt: Thank you for sculpting my manuscript into its final form.

Larry Kreider: Thank you for giving me the freedom to write.

My mentors — Dr. Vernon Grounds, Mother Teresa, Tony Campolo, Immaculée Ilibagiza, Rich Van Pelt, Elisabeth Elliot, Oswald Chambers, Kim Phuc, C. S. Lewis, Rachel Joy Scott, Richard Foster, Jack Larson, Elvis, Bono, Johnny Cash, Bob Dylan, and Gil Larribas: Thank you for showing me the ways of **grace** *and* **truth.**

Dan Brake: Thank you for the innumerable phone calls. You totally "get it."

Tom Lynch: Thank you for making me laugh on Thursday mornings. ✓

YOU CAN MAKE A DIFFERENCE

SERVING THE WORLD OUTSIDE OF YOURSELF

*What makes you qualified to help a person
who has been knocked down in a car accident?
There's only one qualification, that you happened
to be there . . . to call the ambulance. That's it.
When you're lying down there, choking on
the road, you're not gonna ask: "Excuse me,
have you got a qualification?"*

—BONO

"LOOK AT me, look at my eyes. I am already dead."

He was on his way to court, uncuffed, to face charges of rape and sodomy. Instead, he brutally assaulted the police officer who was escorting him, took her gun, and went looking for the judge. He was not in a hurry. He ran into a deputy, handcuffed him, and locked him in a closet. He went to the judge's chambers, handcuffed an attorney and a secretary, and secured them there. He walked calmly to the courtroom, shot and killed the judge and his court reporter, and then killed a deputy sheriff on the street outside while making his escape. On the run, and the focus of the largest manhunt in Georgia history, he confronted a federal agent in his home, took his gun and his life, and stole his truck.

He was a dead man . . . just waiting to die. ✓

She was a twenty-six-year-old single mom who was working as a waitress and taking classes at a medical-technician school. Her five-year-old daughter was in the custody of an aunt. Four years earlier, her husband had died in her arms, the victim of a knife fight and stabbing. She was familiar with pain, failure, and despair. As a troubled teen, she had used hard drugs and had been arrested for various crimes. As a young adult, she was charged with drunken driving and assault.[1]

Then her life got turned around. She experienced love, hope, and acceptance at a drug rehabilitation center. She found God's forgiveness and discovered a reason for living beyond her present meager existence and the tragic memories of her past. Her life began to change as she focused on loving her daughter. She reached outside of herself through the compelling pull of God's love and discovered the satisfying fulfillment of simply loving one other person.

In spite of her failures, broken dreams, and dashed hopes, this once troubled soul, the most *ordinary* of people, somehow changed the world. Something new was born in her when she allowed herself to receive God's love and the acceptance of others. It was not a dramatic, immediate change-of-life experience, but a growing calm, an increased perception that God was aware of her. As she cared for her daughter, her spirit softened, she experienced a sense of hope, and she felt that she had a reason to live.

Her reason for living was about to be tested . . . in the most extreme way.

When fugitive Brian Nichols placed a gun to Ashley Smith's ribs and forced his way into her apartment, she thought her life was over. She later said her first thought was that Nichols was going to strangle her. Instead, he took her into the bathroom, tied her up with masking tape, an extension cord, and a curtain, put a towel over her head, and took a shower.

Later, he wanted to talk. He untied Ashley and began asking her questions. She talked about the things that mattered most to her. She spoke of her daughter, Paige, and the tragic loss of her husband. She told Brian about her new faith in God, and the disappointment Paige would feel if she didn't show up for a visit on Saturday morning.

"Can I go and see Paige?" she asked.

"No."

Looking for some source of comfort, Ashley asked if she could read.

Brian allowed her to get her Bible and a copy of Rick Warren's book *The Purpose Driven Life*. She read aloud from chapter 33. Brian asked her to stop and read it again, so she did:

> We serve God by serving others. In our self-serving cul-
> ture with its "me-first" mentality, acting like a servant is
> not a popular concept. Jesus, however, measured great-
> ness in terms of service, not status. God determines
> your greatness by how many people you serve, not how
> many people serve you. God shaped you for service, not

for self-centeredness. Without a servant's heart, you will be tempted to misuse your shape for personal gain.[2]

Brian was moved by these words and began to talk again. Later, Ashley described what he said to her during those tense yet intimate moments. "He thought that I was an angel sent from God. And that I was his sister and he was my brother in Christ. And that he was lost and God led him right to me to tell him that he had hurt a lot of people. And the families—the people—to let him know how they felt, because I had gone through it. He looked at pictures of my family. He asked me if he could look at them and hold them."[3]

A bond, a trust—an unlikely connection—was developing between Ashley and Brian.

Brian hid his guns and asked Ashley to help him hide the truck he had stolen from the federal agent he had killed. She drove her car while he drove the truck. He allowed her to take her cell phone, but she didn't call the police. She wanted to further build his trust in her, so she made no attempt to escape. She wanted him to surrender, she did not want anyone else to get hurt, and she very much wanted to see Paige.

They drove back to Ashley's apartment. Brian said something about being hungry, and Ashley cooked him breakfast.

He was overwhelmed. "Wow—real butter, pancakes?"

They talked some more, about God and their lives, and Brian agreed to let Ashley see Paige. He gave her forty dollars and offered to rehang the curtain he had taken down to tie her with.

She offered him hope and a reason to live.

"You're here in my apartment for some reason. You got out of the courthouse with police everywhere, and you don't think that's a miracle? You don't think you're supposed to be sitting here right in front of me listening to me tell you, you know, your reason here? Your miracle could be that you need to—you need to be caught for this. You need to go to prison and you need to share the word of God with them, with all the prisoners there."[4]

Brian asked Ashley what she thought he should do.

She told him, "I think you should turn yourself in. If you don't, lots more people are going to get hurt. And you're probably going to die."

In the end, the bloody shoot-out with the police never happened. There was no kicked-in door with a super-cop taking command of the situation and overpowering the criminal, like in the movies. It was not dramatic, and there was no struggle. There was no fight left in the man.

If anything, it was anticlimactic.

Just before noon on the day after his escape from the courthouse, Brian Nichols gave himself up to the police, waving a white T-shirt in surrender. There was no need for drama, because a quiet work had begun in Brian Nichols's heart. It was the work of a broken woman who was willing to reveal her fears and her painful past. She was transparent enough to talk about her love for her precious daughter and her new relationship with God. ✓

Such stories don't usually end this way. Many times the hostages die. So what made the difference in this case?

How did this young woman capture the heart of a killer who had evaded authorities for twenty-six hours while beating or shooting anyone who got in his way?

The ordinary and the commonplace made the difference, not the extraordinary.

Wouldn't you think that Ashley Smith would be the least qualified person to make a difference in the life of a killer? Wouldn't you think that a trained counselor, minister, or reformed ex-con would have been the expert of choice to intervene?

But Ashley was the one who made the difference, and I believe that you can make a difference in your world as well.

ॐ

Three things in this remarkable story are common elements in the lives of people who make a difference in the world.

First, Ashley made a choice to *redeem the immediate moment.* She acted in a way that brought good to everyone caught in this grim situation. She was nearly overwhelmed with fear, but she pushed through her anxiety. Despite the crushing weight of life-threatening circumstances, she chose obedience over fear and hope over hopelessness. She responded to Brian in a way that rescued and redeemed him from his bondage to pain, hatred, violence, and despair.

Making a difference begins with a choice—often a hard choice—to act for the good of something or someone beyond ourselves. I call this "redemptive action."

Second, Ashley *developed a relationship.* She connected with Brian Nichols on a personal level by sharing how her tragic life had turned around. She told her story in a real and authentic way, offered him hope, and made him pancakes with real butter. Though, on one level, she may have felt hatred toward him, she did not preach condemnation to him. She cared for him, even though he was a brutal murderer.

This was a "reconciling relationship."

Making a difference always involves a personal, real connection with someone whom we may not even know, like, or choose to be with. Reconciliation brings hatred and hostilities to an end and replaces them with harmonious relationships.

By the time Ashley left to visit Paige on Saturday morning, Brian had begun to find something that he had lost long ago. It was the beginning of restoration to a fellow human being that he had once thought of killing, and to the God that she reintroduced him to. Out of Ashley's brokenness, and from the seeds of hope planted in her by God, he discovered his own hope of finding God and of being reconciled with him.

Third, Ashley encouraged Brian to *seek spiritual restoration.* This is the natural conclusion to taking redemptive action and building a reconciling relationship. This is most powerful when expressed though our brokenness and our connection with God.

When Ashley chose to act "redemptively," she related genuinely to Brian. When Brian encountered an authentic, non-condemning relationship, his heart was able to respond to Ashley and to the God she was getting to know. In the end, she helped to set Brian free to begin a path of spiritual restoration.

I call this "restoration to God and to your fellow man."

Seven gut-wrenching hours in the lives of a single mom and a wanted murderer—from 2:00 A.M. to 9:00 A.M.—was all it took for God to transform the ordinary into the extraordinary.

That was God's plan for their lives.

God has a plan for your life as well.

Will you discover it and take hold of it? √

You are here for a purpose. God did not place you in life's audience merely to observe, nor did he give you an audience for whom you must perform. He placed you on center stage in the midst of the world he created, exactly where he wanted you. People, circumstances, triumph, and tragedy will act upon you.

What will you do?

Will you become the difference maker that God designed you to be?

Someone once said that the future belongs to those who live intensely in the present. Was that person talking about you?

Am I expecting you to have already arrived? No, not at all. Like you, I am still on the journey, and so is Ashley Smith. She is a recovering drug user, and at the point that she met Brian Nichols, she was on the road to getting clean, but was still having a hard time letting go of drugs.

I was very interested in reading the story that came with the following headline:

HOSTAGE GAVE GUNMAN DRUGS

Yes, Ashley Smith, the unlikely angel, gave drugs to Brian Nichols.

When I read that, my first thought was, *That is not the profile of a difference maker. The opening story of my book has been destroyed! What will I do now?* Then I took a deep breath, looked deeper, read Ashley's book, and watched her TV interviews before drawing a final conclusion.

Here's what I discovered.

Brian Nichols asked for marijuana and Ashley didn't have any, but she had a small amount of methamphetamine. She thought that by giving Brian drugs she might curry favor. When he asked her to take them as well, she declined. If she was going to die, she decided, she was going to die drug free, for the sake of her daughter. That's when Ashley finally kicked her habit. She couldn't bear the thought of disappointing Paige one more time by having traces of drugs in her blood at the time of her death. If not taking the drugs meant that Brian killed her, she was willing to accept it.[5]

She was finally willing to be clean at any cost.

She had discovered a reason to live, and if it cost her life to love her daughter in this way, she was willing to trust the outcome to God. ✓

REFLECTIONS

Take a few moments to reflect on these questions and write down your thoughts. The insights you gain by meditating on each response will help you personalize the principles of this chapter.

What are the "possibilities within" that you want to discover?

What is one small thing you will do today to make your ordinary life extraordinary?

Where does God fit in your equation to "change the world?" ✓

2

NO LITTLE PEOPLE

IT'S NOT WHERE YOU'RE FROM;
IT'S WHERE YOU'RE GOING

*I love working with seventeen- and eighteen-
year-old kids, because I feel I can make a
difference in their lives.*

—DAVE WANNSTEDT, HEAD FOOTBALL COACH,
UNIVERSITY OF PITTSBURGH

LET'S TAKE A CLOSER look at the concept of making a difference.
It's a phrase that rolls off our lips with incredible frequency these
days. We hear it on the radio and television and see it in the
newspaper and on bumper stickers.

"You can make a difference in this year's taxes if you call
by December 31."

"Making a Difference: American Soldier Returns to Iraq to Help the Children."

"Picnic for homeless makes a difference with food, fun, and clothing."

"Parents Make a Difference."

Everywhere we turn, it seems, there's somebody telling us that we can make a difference. We talk about making a difference all the time, but do we really know what it means? Can an ordinary person such as you or me actually live an extraordinary life? Can ordinary people change the world?

I think so.

In 1974, Dr. Francis Schaeffer, a renowned philosopher and theologian of the twentieth century, published a book titled *No Little People.* To summarize his thoughts in a sentence: In God's sight there are no "little people" and no "little places"—only individuals who offer their lives in consecrated moments of obedience to God. When they do this, he gives them the power to influence the flow of an entire generation.

Schaeffer also spoke of how we so often belittle ourselves: "I am so limited. I am such a small person, so limited in talents (or energy or psychological strength or knowledge) that what I do is not really important."[1]

Have you ever been there?

I have. I've asked:

"Does anything I do really matter?"

"Is my life having an impact?"

"Am I making a difference?"

Schaeffer counters that view with a godly perspective by saying, "The Bible . . . has quite a different emphasis: With God there are no little people."[2]

I have been inclined to discount my own influence and abilities. I'm the baby of the family, the youngest of three boys born to Depression-era parents. My dad was born in 1908 in Brewer, Maine. He was a lumberjack with a sixth-grade education, and he was prone to high blood pressure, strokes, and heart attacks, but he worked three jobs. My mom was born in 1914 in Willoughby Township, Ontario, Canada. She was a seamstress with an eighth-grade education, and she carried chronic bronchitis and a displaced hip to her grave. Not a single ancestor in my family tree attended college, dating back to 1620 when they arrived on the *Mayflower* at Plymouth, Massachusetts. My genealogical history suggests that I come from a long line of "little people." ✓

I was born in Lincoln, Maine. To find the backwoods shack of my birth, get on any highway in Maine and drive north. Eventually, every paved road converges into a single bumpy dirt lane that leads into the mountains. When you stop seeing moose, deer, and bear, you arrive at a small clearing with a sign:

LINCOLN, MAINE   1 MILE

END OF CIVILIZATION   1.1 MILES

You could say that I come from a "little place."

I've given you an accurate account of my lineage and taken a tender jab at my birthplace. (Actually, the end of civilization is 1.2 miles away.) I was born into a backwoods world and grew up in a small 1950s town in upstate New York. This small and mostly safe world centered on family, neighborhood, work, and faith. There wasn't anything else. ✓

In the "little world" of my past, it never occurred to me that what I did would ever take me anywhere *big*. If you would have told me that one day I would have connections with people at the epicenter of world power—the White House—and that I would have occasion to meet and get to know a variety of prominent people, I wouldn't have believed you. In my mind, such opportunities were reserved for people who were gifted, powerful, and important.

As I reflect on my experiences, it seems I just "showed up for life" every day, with as much concern for others as I had for myself, and God used those opportunities to do some interesting work.

After graduating in 1970 with my class of forty-eight from Dover High School in Dover Plains, New York, I spent the next six and a half years working with profoundly disabled individuals at Wassaic Developmental Center in Wassaic, New York. I fed hungry mouths, carried crippled children, and bathed deformed teens and adults.

During that time, I attended Dutchess Community College in Poughkeepsie—another not-so-big place. As I searched for a career path, I frequently found myself listening to my buddies as they shared their stories, problems, and fears with me. Somehow it was evident that I was approachable and interested in their lives and had something to offer them.

After community college, I transferred to the State University of New York at Albany to get a degree in psychology. My time at SUNY was not made memorable by the classes I took or the psychological theories I studied, but by the people I met. Those friendships and experiences shaped me and enlarged my little world.

I lived for two years with six roommates—three New York City Jews and two other upstate New York Gentile boys. We learned from, contributed to, and accepted each other, and I was best man at my Jewish roommate's wedding.

I was recruited as the only white player on an all-black intramural flag football team. We stood together when issues of race arose with an opposing all-white team. My roommates nicknamed me "Brother" for participating in this league.

I spent hours listening as my friends shared their brokenness with me. I had the intimidating task of moderating the reunion of a close female friend with her angry boyfriend at 2:30 one morning after he had driven a hundred miles to see her. I was privileged to help restore this broken relationship.

To pay my way through college, I drove the 180-mile round trip from Albany to Wassaic every weekend to work twenty hours at the developmental center. Then, in 1976, I left cloudy Albany and headed to sunny Colorado to begin a master's program in counseling at Denver Seminary.

In Denver, I was introduced to the world of incarcerated teenagers. My degree program required me to volunteer ten hours each week at the youth lockup. There I was matched with a sixteen-year-old boy and immediately realized that I could make a difference in the world of one troubled kid. So compelling was our relationship, and my love for him, that I applied to Youth Guidance and became the chaplain of the Denver juvenile hall for four years. You'll meet some of my "juvy" kids in the pages of this book.

From Denver, I moved to Columbus, Ohio, in 1981—not
for the scenery or sunshine, but for an opportunity to open a
Youth Guidance program there. If I wanted to have an impact on
these inner-city kids, I thought, it would be best if I lived *in* the
city, so I did. For the next seven years my wife, Rita, and I built
relationships with kids, parents, schools, the courts, and churches
while developing a comprehensive outreach to disadvantaged and
troubled kids.

In 1988, I left Youth Guidance to become executive director of
The Gathering, a faith-based program that addresses the moral,
ethical, and spiritual needs of business, professional, and government leaders. One day I was driving a van full of inner-city kids,
and the next day I was meeting a business owner for lunch. I felt
overwhelmed by the challenges of my new career, but I had a
sense that this was now where God wanted me to be.

One weekly small group for men soon became two, and then
three. As a man's life and marriage were changed, his family and
business relationships changed as well. One person introduced
me to another. A clothier introduced me to a company president,
who introduced me to a banker, who introduced me to a mort-
gage broker, and so on. Our attendance exploded.

One "small" inspirational breakfast for 350 men became
The Spring Gathering Breakfast (with 750 in attendance), the
Ohio Prayer Breakfast (with 2,000 men and women), and the
Columbus Leadership Prayer Breakfast (with 4,000 in attendance). The mayor of Columbus, the governor of Ohio, U.S.
senators, and congressional representatives participated in our
programs as they saw the transforming work being accomplished
by God in individual lives. The Gathering became a regular stop-
ping place for leaders and dignitaries.

Our speakers had authentic, powerful stories to tell. Adolph
Coors IV spoke of the kidnapping and murder of his father and

the impact it had on his life. Tony Campolo touched us deeply with his compelling stories of the poorest of the poor in Haiti. Darrell Scott told of the horrific loss of his daughter Rachel in the killings at Columbine High School. Each had a unique view on the power of redemptive action and the ability of one person to make a difference in the life of another.

We invited President Clinton to speak to us, but he declined. The same thing happened with President Bush, but he sent in his place Jim Towey, director of the White House Office of Faith-Based and Community Initiatives and, later, White House chief of staff Andrew Card, Jr. When Jim Towey was with us, he and I moderated a community-wide roundtable discussion with faith-based leaders, and we toured a highly successful inner-city program called Urban Concern.

Jim Towey and I became friends, and at his invitation, I participated in the inaugural White House Conference on Faith-Based Initiatives, held in Washington, D.C. I was seated in the second row and had the privilege of meeting President Bush there.

What took me from Lincoln, Maine, to the White House was not a desire to pursue the halls of power and influence. What took me there was a desire to touch the world around me and serve the world beyond me.

I sometimes wonder where God will lead me next. Lately, I have worked with children and poor families in the small villages of Cielo and Nazaret in the Dominican Republic, but that's a story for later in the book. ✓

I became aware of my limitations and weaknesses at an early age. If some good has come from my life, or if I have made a significant impact on the life of another person, I know it is because I've invited God to be "the difference maker" who could truly offer hope, help, and freedom to those I've befriended.

Making a difference begins when we reach beyond ourselves to other people in ways that invite God to be present as well. When we deliberately *include* God in our day-to-day lives, we share in the beginning of a miracle—the reconciliation and restoration of people to God and to one another.

As I write of this greatest miracle of all, I'm well aware that on any given day I may not feel much like a difference maker. There are days when I'm just too comfortable and apathetic to want to make a difference. When this happens, I realize I have diminished myself and missed out on some great opportunities. I've found it to be generally true that we tend to limit ourselves, our world, and our vision for life in many ways. We all have a tendency to create the world in our own image, and then we ask others to conform to our image, desires, wants, and goals.

In his book *Against the Night,* Chuck Colson writes, "[We] are creatures of evolution: polyestered discomaniacs became yuppies snorting cocaine in the bathrooms of brass-and-fern eateries, then evolved into leotard-clad health freaks sipping Perrier at the helm of computerized exercycles, who then slumped into today's couch potatoes, ordering pizza delivered with a rental movie. Propped in front of a VCR, this self-indulgent species enjoys life without its inconveniences."[3]

I have never snorted cocaine—or worn a leotard!—but I admit that the couch potato image is all too familiar. Colson's point, however, is not that watching TV or ordering a pizza is bad, but that we've become enslaved to our conveniences and our comfort zones. We create artificial worlds around ourselves that serve our needs—and these small worlds confine us. These comfortable walls, reassuring boundaries, and coddling prison bars prevent us from becoming who we truly are.

Breaking out of our comfort zones helps us to expand and become more capable of making a difference in the world. We begin to break free as we open ourselves to the world and to God. Stepping onto unfamiliar turf, in a world with an ever-expanding learning curve, can be frightening, and it requires that we exercise our faith in God. ✓

∾

I was struck by an article in the *Columbus Dispatch* following the deadly tsunami that took the lives of more than 260,000 people:

KNOWLEDGE OF NATURE MAY HAVE SAVED TRIBES

> Anthropologists think that ancient knowledge of the movement of wind, sea, and birds might have saved the five indigenous tribes on the Indian archipelago of the Andaman and Nicobar islands from the tsunami that hit the Asian coastline on December 26. They can smell the wind. They can gauge the depth of the sea with the sound of their oars. They live the most ancient, nomadic lifestyle known to man, frozen in their Paleolithic past.[4]

While tens of thousands of people from "advanced cultures" died oblivious to the coming disaster in their region, these five "prehistoric tribes" suffered very little loss of life. Their lives were saved by their intimate awareness of the wind and sea, and the movements of the birds, fish, and animals upon which they depend.

In other words, the most technologically educated cultures were oblivious to the basic meteorological signs around them. They missed what was plainly obvious to the least technologically attuned people on the planet. They missed the message of the birds and the sea that could have saved their lives. The people from ancient cultures understood the unique way in which nature communicated the coming tragedy. They were in tune and in touch with their world, and it saved their lives.

These ancient tribes vividly illustrate our need to remain in tune with the world around us. Only then, by gauging the depth of life with the sound of our spiritual oars, can we survive unseen waves of destruction such as self-absorption, indifference, affluence, apathy, religiosity, materialism, convenience, independence, tolerance, envy, self-fulfillment, political correctness, bitterness, busyness, idleness, bias, prejudice, and pride.

Albert Einstein said, "The real problem is in the hearts and minds of men. It is not a problem of physics but of ethics. It is easier to denature plutonium than to denature the evil spirit of man."[5] In other words, to reach beyond ourselves violates a part of our nature that continually seeks self-satisfaction. It requires a new ethic, an ethic of godly service. Opening up to the world outside of yourself may mean beginning to put this new ethic into action.

Perhaps you need to move out of your own version of Lincoln, Maine.

Maybe it would help you to get outside of the circles of people you usually hang out with. Perhaps you need to read something different, try a new hobby, learn a new skill, or invest in the life of another person.

Just changing your physical environment and the things that you do will not be sufficient. The comfort zone that you've carved out for yourself, the "world according to you" that you live by, can easily become a god that rules your life. This god limits you, and that's why I speak about opening up to the God outside of yourself.

What form does this "inner god" take for you?

I'll be honest—for me, it's the god of fear. It's a lingering cold-ness that shows up before I get out of bed in the morning. It's a doubt in my abilities. This god says, "Harvey, why would anyone want to follow you? You're an outsider," or, "What do you have to say that would interest anyone else?"

This god says that there's a big, bad world out there that is popu-lated by people who are more intelligent and more gifted than I am. It's a temptation to settle for second best or for just getting by. Fear sometimes shows up with his roommate: *second-guessing.*

"Well, if only you would have . . ."

"Why'd you do it that way?"

"I told you that wasn't going to work."

To offset their taunts, I focus so much on planning the next moment, the next interaction, or the next event, that I don't live in the moment and I miss the present.

During one of those doubting, fearful times, I asked God to strengthen me in my moments of weakness. What he said to me may encourage you as well:

> *Stop living under fear.*
> *Stop living for results. Stop trying to measure up.*
> *Live. Love. Live in the moment. Live for me.*
> *Touch the lonely. Touch the hurting.*
> *Stop thinking about yourself.*
> *Experience my presence.*
> *Forgive.*
> *Forget.*

Love.
Live.
Live today.
Live in the moment.

For many people, the god of self takes the form of various plea-sures—food, travel, TV, drugs, sex, sports, shopping. Pleasure is another comfort zone that asks to be indulged. We substitute our inner worlds of desire for reality as we satiate ourselves to mask the emptiness within. It's a self-focused, self-centered, self-medi-cating world, but we can always make a different choice.✓

ACTIONS

May I challenge you to take one small step of redemptive action? Will you release your hold on the god of self-preoccupation?

Most of us live in a world that we've created for ourselves. If we could stop being so preoccupied with ourselves, our worlds would instantly expand and bring us closer to God and to one another.

In short, stop living for other people's approval; stop living up to someone else's standards; and stop thinking so much about yourself. It's a tough assignment, because our world tells us that the universe begins and ends with us.

But in "the world according to us," we remain little people. In the world according to God—the one true God, who is out-side of us—we can change the world.

1. *Write down one "little thing" in your life that is keeping you from reaching your potential.*

2. *Write down one "big thing" you would like to do that you have not yet attempted.*

3

THE PATH LESS TAKEN

CROSSING THE RIVER OF HUMAN EXISTENCE

*I will lead the blind by ways they have not
known, along unfamiliar paths I will guide them;
I will turn the darkness into light before them
and make the rough places smooth.*

—ISAIAH 42:16

IT'S A SCARY THING to journey with God, because we're always on his turf. He knows the terrain, the reasons for the experiences we encounter, and our final destination far better than we do. He invites us to leave the known for the unknown and the certain for the uncertain. If we want to be where God is, we must follow him. In venturing along these paths, we learn to rely on him. As we take the next—often hesitant—step, he lights the way and guides us over the rough places. We have to learn that God has engineered the path we are on.

God's pathways are designed to bring fullness to us and to others. Ashley Smith had her own specific pathway to travel, and you have yours. Which way will you turn when you face the next fork in the road? Will you step into the darkness in response to your Maker's voice? Or will you pause, turn aside, and let your doubts and inner fears direct you?

God is our guide on the journey of life. He offers no quick-fix, superficial, seven-step self-help program that can be ordered online or by calling an 800-number in the middle of the night. He offers no shortcuts, but he does point the direction and place stepping stones specifically where our feet are to fall.

I believe that whether we are five, twenty-five, fifty-five, or one hundred and five, we will wake up one day to the reality that life is a journey across the river of human existence. We stand on one side and realize that we are destined to cross to the other side. Or we may discover that we are partway across but don't know where we are going!

The way that we cross the river forms our character, and our *destination* shapes our *destiny.* We are going to God, and we leave behind an all-important legacy.

I will mention fear and doubt many times in this book, because I am so familiar with them—they are part of my life. I can let them stop me in my tracks or turn me to God. When I turn to God, I find that he is always present to lead and guide me. Sometimes I see him, and sometimes I don't. He doesn't appear at my command, but I know that he never leaves me.

I'm often reminded of this by the words of Ezekiel, an Old Testament Jewish prophet:

> I saw water coming out from under the threshold of the temple, . . . under the south side of the temple, south of the altar. . . . [The man] led me through water that was

ankle-deep . . . and led me through water that was knee-deep . . . and led me through water that was up to the waist. . . . He said to me, "Where the river flows, everything will live." (Ezekiel 47:1-9)

An ever-present, all-knowing, wise, loving, and faithful God leads us through the waters of life at every level: ankle-deep, knee-deep, waist-deep, neck-deep, or over our heads. He is with us in the calm pools and in the rushing current. He knows that only as we step forward in faith to follow his lead will our lives be worth living. ✓

I believe that God places twelve stepping stones before us as we cross the river of human existence. They are not in plain sight, but lie below the surface of the water, forming the pathway that God wants for us to travel.

Like all worthwhile things, they must be sought, discovered, valued, understood, acted upon, and passed on to others. As God reveals these stones to us, he answers questions; this makes life worthwhile and turns hope into action. Our questions draw us forward, and God meets us at each stepping stone to answer the significant questions of our lives.

These are the stones we all encounter, and the questions that lead us to them:

1. *Destiny.* What happens to me when I die? What is my final fate?

2. *Call.* What is God saying to me? Is God asking me to do something?

3. *Vision.* Is it possible to see the future when it isn't here yet?

4. *Purpose.* Why do I exist? Why did God place my DNA on planet earth?

5. *Mission.* What am I supposed to do with my life? What is my assignment?

6. *Gifts and Abilities.* What do I do well? How did God make me different from everyone else?

7. *Core Values and Priorities.* What is all-important? What guides my life? What am I willing to die for? What makes life worth living?

8. *Strategy.* What is my plan for pursuing a significant life?

9. *Goals.* How do I measure progress? How do I evaluate success?

10. *Difference Making.* Is my life expressed in redemptive action? Do I restore others to God and to their world?

11. *Legacy.* What will I leave behind when I'm gone? Will it reflect God?

12. *Transformed World.* Does my life change others for the better? Will the world be a better place because I passed through? ✓

It isn't possible to fully address these issues in a single book, so it's important for you to remember that God has your life in his hands. All he asks you to do is to take the next step.

The first step is to *listen for God's voice.*

If you're like most people, you may not have a lot of confidence about hearing God speak to you. I love how Dr. Jay Kesler, president emeritus of Taylor University, once responded to a criticism of his work: "I prefer to do what I do poorly, over what you don't do at all!" Like Jay, you may have to begin your listening by doing it poorly. So what? Just begin!

The psalmist says that God "will give you the desires of your heart" (Psalm 37:4). But it could also be translated, "God will cause your heart to desire a thing." In other words, God places desires in our hearts, and then he satisfies them. Ask God to help you listen to your true desires. When your heart desires to listen to God, he will fulfill your longing.

Many things get in the way of listening to God. One of the obstacles is, or can be, religion. By religion, I mean the institutions created by man to build favor with God, or an expression of belief in God through conduct and ritual. Remember that religion and ritual are not identical to a relationship with God.

Bono, the lead singer of the rock group U2, says, "One of the things I picked up from my father and my mother was the sense that religion often gets in the way of God."[1] Bono's parents allowed the differences between their Protestant and Catholic traditions to get in the way of their relationship with one another, with others, and with the God they said they worshiped. This wounded Bono's early desire to know God, and it became a handicap that he had to overcome to discover his faith. ✓

Fear also gets in the way of our listening to God. It often causes us to stop short of truly listening for God's voice. This can happen, for example, when we place our faith in religion instead of

God. Here are some of the questions that hinder us from asking God to speak to us:

How can I find time to do it?

What if I'm not important to God?

What about all the thoughts that keep running through my mind?

How can I know that God is talking to me? What if I'm just hearing my own thoughts?

What if God doesn't show up or speak to me?

Oh, my goodness . . . what if he does?

What if I don't like what he says?

At one time or another, I've asked all of these questions, so I'm very familiar with them. I've had to set them aside to discover a deeper, more meaningful spiritual life. When I set aside my fear, I discover that God shows up and he does speak. Although he may not answer each question to my immediate satisfaction, I'm well aware that he is there.

On June 8, 2005, for example, I got up at 4:30 A.M. with one agenda for the next sixty minutes: I was going to listen to God. No, I don't get up at this hour every day, but that morning I did.

It was scary . . . one-on-one with God, just listening.

It was forty-five minutes of silence, distracting thoughts, and mounting pressures from my approaching day. At 5:15 A.M., I heard God say, in my spirit, "Be still and know that I am God."

I was underwhelmed. I had read this passage from Psalms before, and I had heard it many times. It is a familiar Scripture passage to a lot of people, and I couldn't see any special message in it for me. With a sigh of disappointment, I thought, *Oh well, time to wake up Rita, grab a second cup of coffee, and go for a workout.*

Throughout the day, I kept thinking about what I had heard and wondering what would happen if I showed up the next morning at the same time and place with a notepad and pen in hand. I wondered whether I was missing something below the surface. I had to find out, and on June 9, God revealed the depths of what he wanted to say to me. I began to write what he spoke in my heart as I reflected on the words, "Be still and know that I am God." Here, and throughout this book, my "poems" are simply my record of what I understood God was saying to me.

Be still
And know that I am God.
Be still.
Be still and I will come to you.
Be still, and do not think.
Be still, and I will be still with you.
Be still.
I am Alpha and Omega, the beginning and the end.
Be still. I am your peace, your joy, your protection,
*   and your salvation.*
Be still. I am Love, Hope, Resurrection, and Life.
Be still. I am the Way, the Truth, and the Life.
Be still. I am the Light of the world.
Be still. I am your provider.
Be still. I AM God.
Be still
And know that I am near.

Be still. I want to speak to you.
Be still and hear my voice.
Be still and feel the touch of my hand.
Be still and I will touch your soul.
Be still and I will work in your life.
Be still so you can drink me in.
Be still and rest in me.
Be still
And discover how I made you.
Be still and Peace will come.
Be still and I will heal you.
Be still and know no fear.
Be still. I have conquered fear, sin, death, and hell.
Be still
And I will take you up into the heavens.
Be still and you will become like me.
Be still and I will fill you with hope.
Be still and experience this moment.
Be still and I will fill you with myself.
Be still and know that before the world was,
I AM.
Be still. I love you.
Be still.

I didn't know what would result from my listening until I listened. I showed up and God showed up.

In this poem, God answered every major question I had about my life, my future, and my pathway across the river of human existence. He said, in effect, "Get on with the journey; get on with your life; I've already handled all of the big stuff. All the rest is small stuff, and you never need to worry about the small stuff. You may not know what you'll be doing in 2010, but you know that I'll be there with you. You don't know when you will die, but you know where I will be when you do. Life was meant to be lived, so go and live it!"

You will not interpret my poem the same way I did, because the message was not for you. I believe that God has a message—many messages—for you, and you will recognize them because they will touch you in a way that nothing else can, and they will have a very personal meaning for you.

All God asks is that you show up. He is waiting to reveal your life's path to you, but he will probably reveal it to you one step at a time. Is that sufficient for you? Will you go into the waters with him to the ankle, knee, waist, or neck? Will you listen for his voice and follow him? ✓

In the following chapters, God will show up numerous times to speak to you—I'm sure of it. In the end, if you choose to embrace all that God has for you, you will become a person of redemptive action who enters into reconciling relationships and transforms the world around you into a greater likeness of God. I cannot think of a better reason for living.

While you are waiting for a message from God that is unique to you, let me offer you another passage from the Bible to encourage you. Listen closely as God speaks:

> What I am commanding you today is not too difficult
> for you or beyond your reach. It is not up in heaven, so
> that you have to ask, "Who will ascend into heaven to
> get it? . . ." No, the word is very near you; it is in your
> mouth and in your heart so you may obey it.
>
> See, I set before you today life and prosperity, death

and destruction. For I command you today to love the
LORD your God, to walk in his ways, and to keep his
commands, decrees, and laws; then you will live and
increase, and the LORD your God will bless you in the
land you are entering to possess. . . .

This day I call heaven and earth as witnesses against
you that I have set before you life and death, blessings
and curses. Now choose life, so that you and your children may live and that you may love the LORD your God,
listen to his voice, and hold fast to him. For the LORD is
your life, and he will give you many years in the land he
swore to give to your fathers, Abraham, Isaac and Jacob.
(Deuteronomy 30:11-20)

The key to understanding what God was saying to me came
when I meditated on his words. What is he saying to *you* in this
passage?

Over time, God will reveal the steps along the path of life that
he has ordained for you. He may intervene in a dramatic, life-
changing, life-threatening event confined to a seven-hour period
as he did with Ashley Smith and Brian Nichols. Or he may guide
you in a life-sustaining, life-enhancing, slowly-revealed course of
action that reshapes a solitary life or touches an entire culture.

Whatever he chooses for you, accept it, embrace it, and expect
surprises along the way. He offers you the path of redemptive
action and reconciling relationships, and he is shining his light
on the next stone that will take you across the river of human
existence. ✓

REFLECTIONS

What river do you need to cross?

4

CHOSEN BY GOD

EMBRACING YOUR DESTINY

God reveals things to us on a
"need to know" basis.

—BRIAN PETERSON

JULY 20, 1969, began unlike any day he had ever known—or
perhaps even imagined. Neil Armstrong, a small-town boy from
Wapakoneta, Ohio, was about to become the first man ever to
leave his footprints on the moon. As he prepared to step onto the
Sea of Tranquillity, six hundred million TV viewers worldwide
were transfixed with anticipation. The impossible was about to
happen. The most dramatic accomplishment of Neil Armstrong,
NASA, and exploration history was but moments away. It was an
intense night of remarkable scientific achievement!

That same day—July 20, 1969—began unlike any day I had ever known or imagined. I was about to participate in my own "unbelievable moment in history." Unable to sleep, I watched the snowy black-and-white picture on the hospital television, hoping to catch a glimpse of Commander Armstrong descending the steps of the Apollo 11 Lunar Module. While the world at large waited for the impossible to happen on the lunar surface, I waited for the impossible to happen in my private world.

My chest had been shaved in anticipation of my scheduled encounter with surgeon Rama P. Coomaraswamy in the operating room at Sharon Hospital in Sharon, Connecticut. They were preparing to remove a mysterious lump from my sternum, one of only eleven such cases reported in the medical journals.

Neil Armstrong was facing a future of unprecedented fame and would forever be known as the first man to walk on the moon. I was about to discover whether I had cancer and how long I would walk on the earth.

I was alone and afraid, and I could see no reason why this should be happening to me. I was the only occupant of the dark hospital room. My ordinary, commonplace world had been radically interrupted by an unwanted and possibly malignant visitor. I had been like every other kid I knew, but that was no longer the case. I contemplated life, death, pain, and the hereafter as I wondered if I would ever have another day like all the days I had lived before.

That day had actually begun like any other day. I had been hiding out from doing my chores, running down to the creek, shooting baskets in the sun, and sweating onto the floor while gulping water at the kitchen sink—mouth to the faucet, no glass required.

As I waited for my mom to chase me out the screen door, she asked, "What's that lump on your chest?"

One day I was healthy, and the next day I had osteochondroma (a rapidly growing, fungating tumor) in my sternum. One day I was playing in the backyard, and the next day a tube was inserted down my nose to make me cough and dislodge the fluids rapidly filling my lungs. One day I was swimming, and the next day I was in intensive care. One day I was earning the President's Physical Fitness Award, and the next day I was wearing a thirteen-inch scar with a fist-sized cavity carved into my chest. One day I didn't have a care in the world, and the next day I was facing months of pain, recovery, and questioning, followed by two unsuccessful plastic surgeries over the next six years.

For Neil Armstrong, it was "one small step for man, one giant leap for mankind." What step was it for this small-town boy living in Wassaic, New York? I was at a disturbing crossroads in my life, engaged in deep questioning as I faced possible death.

I have yet to meet anyone who hasn't experienced some difficult crossroads in his or her life. It's a common condition in our world. I've come to believe that God sends such events to draw us away from the surface realities of our lives to a deeper look into the source, reason, and destiny of our existence. I think that God really does reveal things to us on a need-to-know basis.

Some days, we feel crushed by the loss of a job, friend, spouse, or child, or by the prospect of our own death. On those days, the foggy, distant life-and-death issues come into focus, and we face our mortality. We are snapped to attention and must ask the difficult whys of life. We often discover the inadequacy of our resources when we are forced to face difficult issues of loss, pain, suffering, death, heaven, and hell. I had life by the tail as a sixteen-year-old kid, but the prospect of cancer suddenly jolted me into asking the ultimate questions.

"What happens when I die?"

"Where am I going?"

"What is my destiny?"

As you have no doubt inferred, I'm still here. The rare and rapidly growing tumor in my chest was thankfully benign, but that teenage experience started my asking tough questions about my life, future, and destiny. Only as we answer challenging questions about our existence do we begin to live meaningfully and become the difference makers we are destined to be.

Perhaps the hardest question I wrestled with during my cancer scare was whether God could be known intimately. Was he a personal God that I could trust and interact with? And was there a personal afterlife, or would I die into some anonymous collective destiny along with millions of other people?

Did what happened to *me* matter? Where did the afterlife fit in? Did I matter to God? These were the questions I was asking, and I'm sure that you have asked similar questions yourself.

Some people believe that we all end up in a universal black hole, as nothing, in nothing, surrounded by nothing. That belief is held, for example, by two famous and oft-quoted people: comedian and filmmaker Woody Allen and French philosopher Albert Camus. In their book *Whatever Happened to the Human Race?* C. Everett Koop and Francis Schaeffer write this about Allen:

> Most people know him as a comedian, but he has thought through where mankind stands after the "religious

answers" have been abandoned. In an article in *Esquire* (May 1977), he says that man is left with "alienation, loneliness [and] emptiness verging on madness. . . . The fundamental thing behind *all* motivation and *all* activity is the constant struggle against annihilation and against death. It's absolutely stupefying in its terror, and it renders anyone's accomplishments meaningless. As Camus wrote, it's not only that *he* (the individual) dies, or that *man* (as a whole) dies, but that you struggle to do a work of art that will last and then you realize that *the universe itself* is not going to exist after a period of time."

Allen sums up his view in his film *Annie Hall* with these words: "Life is divided into the horrible and the miserable."[1] ✓

Woody Allen and Albert Camus are not alone in believing that our fate is a collective future of nothingness—that we will occupy a cosmic graveyard that itself will vanish in time. But I cannot accept their conclusions. I simply do not believe that you and I, and all that we do, are meaningless. I don't believe that the baby who just came into the world doesn't really matter, or that the hugs we give and receive are worthless, or that the sum total of all our life experiences is either horrible or miserable.

According to such a nihilistic perspective, we exist only in time and space, and we carry no significance with us today, tomorrow, or forever. Supposedly, there is no God and we are mere protoplasm, dust motes with a few moving parts of evolved machinery that will be consumed by an impersonal universe. My heart cries out against this negative outlook, telling me that I was designed and created for a specific purpose. Nihilism simply cannot be justified by the world in which we live. I knew it in my heart as a sixteen-year-old, and I know it in more definite and defensible ways today. ✓

I have come to believe in an alternate view of my destiny—that God can be known and that I have a personal existence. I discovered that God does not leave us to grope in the dark until we discover something.

God reveals himself to us.

The infinite, living, loving, and personal God of creation stoops down to make himself known:

> What may be known about God is plain to [mankind], because God has made it plain to them. For since the creation of the world God's invisible qualities—his eternal power and divine nature—have been clearly seen, being understood from what has been made. (Romans 1:19-20)

My life experience confirms what this passage tells me. There are times and seasons, sunrise and sunset, order, structure, and glorious beauty all around me. There is love. All people innately search to know where they came from and where they are going. They reflect on their own experiences and those of others. Evolved dust motes would be incapable of doing any of this.

When I go back to the beginning of God's revelation of himself in Scripture, I'm reminded of something else as well. Genesis 1 tells me that you and I were created in God's image. We bear God's mark as truly as a painting bears the signature of the artist. God planned and longed for our existence. We are not accidents, mistakes, or afterthoughts; we were wanted, and we have a purpose and a personal destiny.

You and I both matter.

Bill and Kathy Peel, authors of *Discover Your Destiny,* sum up my thoughts very well:

> Destiny is not something reserved for the famous or fabulously gifted. Every single human being has been specifically designed for his or her appearance in history, and God did the designing. We are not a blank slate to be written on, a lump of clay to be molded by outside, often conflicting forces. We come into this world pre-designed by God.[2]

When we embrace the understanding that destiny is not collective and impersonal, but God's plan for you and me personally, a world of extraordinary possibilities opens up.

In fact, God desires to use you and me for great things. I mean *really great things!*

In *My Utmost for His Highest,* Oswald Chambers writes:

> Our Lord's . . . purpose is not the development of a man; His purpose is to make a man exactly like Himself, and the characteristic of the Son of God is self-expenditure. If we believe in Jesus, it is not what we gain, but what He pours through us that counts. It is not that God makes us beautifully rounded grapes, but that He squeezes the sweetness out of us. Spiritually, we cannot measure our life by success, but only by what God pours through us, and we cannot measure that at all.[3]

If what Chambers writes is true, God will provide the resources and the life experiences necessary for us to arrive at our intended destination. When I care for others, I do so in partnership with God. You and I always operate in the realm of the extraordinary, because God is with us each step of the way! It isn't the size of what I do that counts, but doing the right thing.

I don't stand alone in this belief. ✓

ACTIONS

DAY ONE: *Take 10, 20 or 30 minutes and simply listen to God. (If you need to, bring a note pad to write down the important "to dos" that slip into your mind. It will happen. Once they're written down, you can forget about them and continue your listening uninterrupted.)*

DAY TWO: *Write down what God says to you, however simple, small, or profound it may be. If you find yourself too distracted, go do something else and come back at another time.*

DAY THREE: *Meditate on what God said to you; write down your thoughts and reflections, however short or long they may be.*

5

PARTNERING WITH GOD

PURSUING YOUR DESTINY

It's not what I do that matters but what a sovereign God chooses to do through me.

—ELIZABETH DOLE

In 1987, I invited a small group of church leaders to plan a community event that would unite congregations in central Ohio for prayer, inspiration, and the mobilization of resources to serve the many needy people in our area. I had some ideas about what we should do, but my friends stopped me dead in my tracks when they suggested that before we made any plans, we should stop and ask God what he wanted us to do.

So we stopped and we prayed. In fact, we met regularly for prayer for the next *three years* before we began to get a sense of what God might have in mind for us. And then, almost as if orchestrated by an offstage director, three of the five members of the group suggested that we invite Billy Graham to come to Columbus for a crusade. When the other two members of our group concurred with this idea, we made some inquiries to the Billy Graham Evangelistic Association and extended an invitation. We followed up our initial effort by securing invitations from 150 other church leaders in central Ohio and sent those to Dr. Graham, as well.

In 1993, six years after I called that first meeting to try to "do something" for the Columbus area, Billy Graham came to our city. By then, our initial group of five friends had grown to a partnership of 923 churches across the upper Midwest, who brought together 175,000 people to hear a message of hope, faith, and service to others from Dr. Graham and several special guest speakers, including Elizabeth Dole, who was then president of the American Red Cross. I still meet people today whose lives were touched by those five days in September 1993.

Little did anyone else know at the time, but when Mrs. Dole's plane touched down at Port Columbus International Airport, bringing her to speak at the Billy Graham Crusade, I had already written her an invitation to come back to Columbus to speak for The Gathering in 1994. I gave her the invitation when I drove her back to the airport after the Crusade, and she graciously accepted. ✓

Elizabeth Dole is undoubtedly a difference maker. Her years of public service have placed her repeatedly on the short list of America's most admired women. She holds a master's degree in education and government from Harvard, as well as a degree from Harvard Law School. Her career distinctions include membership in the Federal Trade Commission and service as secretary of transportation under President Ronald Reagan and secretary of labor under President George H. W. Bush. She ran for president herself in 2000, and today she is a U.S. senator from North Carolina.

Before Rita and I hosted Mrs. Dole for the Billy Graham Crusade, we had not met her, so we had a lot of questions. Would she be an "ordinary person," genuine and transparent? Or would she reflect the attitudes of privilege and power that are common to many who have achieved her stature in society?

Both times she came to Columbus, in 1993 and 1994, she arrived late in the day and hungry, following meetings, speaking engagements, and travel delays that included lost luggage. In the midst of these difficult and demanding circumstances of delays, tight timelines, fatigue, and pressure, her character and grace were revealed. She was remarkably kind and gentle, and as interested in our lives as we were in hers. She listened and expressed a humility not commonly found in people of such prominence and influence. In all the behind-the-scenes interactions, in tight quarters, vehicles, and pre-event meeting rooms, she exemplified all the qualities that she would later address in her speeches.

What was the source of her gentle demeanor and warm character? What made her public persona and her private life congruent? We discovered that Mrs. Dole was guided by a humble and profound faith in a God who cares about and is involved in the concerns of all mankind.

I was struck when she said, "It is not what I do that matters, but what a sovereign God chooses to do through me. God doesn't want worldly successes. He wants my heart in submission to him. The world is ripe and ready, I believe, for men and women who recognize that they are not immune to the predicaments of the day, men and women who are willing to accept the privilege of serving, and who are ready to see that the providence of God may have brought them to such a time as this."[1]

What time is it for you? Where has God placed you? Are you on a large stage where you are viewed by the masses, or on a small, obscure stage similar to countless other small stages, where you are largely unseen?

The value of our lives is not determined by the size of the stage, but by how our lives affect other people on whatever stage we've been given. Sometimes the results are immediate and obvious, and sometimes they are not known for fifty years. It is easy to see the impact that Elizabeth Dole has had on many lives for many years.

She just may be the exception.

God may want to use you differently. God may want the results of your life to be revealed slowly over time and hidden from most people. If so, you'll join me and most of the human race. Or your life may more closely follow the path of another woman named Elisabeth.

Elisabeth Elliot and her husband, Jim, were just out of college when they went as missionaries to the Waodani Indians of Ecuador in the 1950s. The Waodani, an Amazon Valley "stone age" people, were more commonly called *Auca* or "naked savages" by the outside world because they were the most violent culture known at that time. Murder, revenge, family vendettas, and blood feuds within the tribe caused half of all Waodani deaths. Another 20 percent lost their lives at the hands of outsiders and other tribes.

Prior to the arrival of the Elliots and four other young American families, the Waodani were on the brink of cultural extinction. The Waodanis' interactions with the Spaniards who came in search of treasure, trade, and conquest, and the other white men who came later in search of rubber and oil, made up a history of distrust, ambush, violence, and death.

Aware of this brutal history, the five couples did extensive research on Waodani culture and language as they made painstaking preparations for their first communication with the tribe. They did not enter this new and very dark world unprepared or unaware of the risks. One wife was pregnant, and several of the couples had young children with them.

In October 1955, the missionaries dropped a package of buttons, ribbons, and rock salt into a small village. Nate Saint, the group's pilot, had devised a system whereby he could slowly circle his plane in the air and gradually let out a rope with a bucket attached so that it slowly settled into a stationary position as it neared the ground. Their first contact with the village happened in this way. For weeks, they continued to drop gifts from the sky, and over time, an increasing number of Waodani came out to receive them.

In January 1956, the men made their first direct, personal contact after landing the plane on a riverbank, setting up camp, and waiting for the natives to arrive.[2] After several days and various sightings, three naked Waodani, two women and a man, emerged from the jungle. Elation mixed with anticipation as two diverse cultures met in an awkward first encounter. When the man expressed interest in the airplane, Nate Saint agreed to take him up for a tour of the area. As the plane skimmed the treetops over the Waodani village, the man, whom the missionaries dubbed "George," shouted and waved to his astonished friends on the ground below.

When the Waodani visitors and the missionaries later parted, the men gave more gifts to the Waodani and felt a growing hope that their evangelistic endeavors would soon be successful.

While Jim Elliot and his companions were touching their destiny for the first time, Elisabeth and the other wives were waiting for word by radio on their progress as they prayed and questioned. Would they become widows? If so, what would they do?

Elisabeth mused, "God's leading was unmistakable up to this point. Each of us knew when we married our husbands that there would never be any question about who came first—God and his work held first place in each life. It became devastatingly meaningful now. The point of decision had been reached. The question of personal safety was wholly irrelevant."[3]

On Sunday, January 8, a group of Waodani warriors left the jungle, crossed the river, and met the five missionary men next to their plane.[4] Back at the base camp, the wives waited by the radio because their husbands were scheduled to call at 4:30 P.M. with news of their big encounter.

At 4:30, the radio remained silent. Had the men been invited to the village? What was it like? What did the Indians give as gifts? How did the children respond to their white skin? The radio didn't even crackle. Were they so preoccupied with the natives that they had forgotten to radio?

No, it was impossible that all five would forget to call.

Something was wrong! The news soon flashed around the world:

FIVE MEN MISSING IN AUCA TERRITORY

A full-scale search and rescue operation was immediately set in motion. When Johnny Keenan, Nate Saint's fellow pilot, flew over the clearing along the river, he spotted Nate's airplane stripped of its fabric exterior. About a quarter-mile downriver from the plane, he saw a body floating facedown in the river.

When the ground party arrived on the scene, they recovered

four of the men's bodies. They had all been speared with Waodani lances, and the spear found in Nate Saint's body had a gospel tract wrapped around the handle. How ironic that the story of God's love would be attached to the instrument of death that pierced Nate's side and ended his life.

Elisabeth and the other wives gathered in a bedroom to wait for word about their husbands, but somehow they knew. They asked unanswerable questions. Who died first? Did they have time to think about our children? How much did they suffer? Were they afraid?

The women received the horrific news with a quiet peace and no tears. It was a supernatural response to the worst news they could have heard. The four men were buried in a common unmarked grave by the river where they died. Ed McCully's body was never recovered, but it had been seen on the beach by a party of Quichua scouts who reached the scene ahead of the rescue party and was believed to have been washed away by the river. One of the Quichuas had removed McCully's watch, which confirmed the identity of the body.

Ten young Americans went into the jungles of Ecuador, seeking to make a difference with their lives. Five of them—Jim Elliot, Nate Saint, Ed McCully, Pete Fleming, and Roger Youderian— met the same fate as 70 percent of the Waodani people they had gone to reach.

But what seemed like a tragic end was also an exciting beginning.

The story of the five martyred missionaries became front-page news around the world, including a ten-page feature in *Life* magazine. The world, stunned by the quick brutality of their deaths, mourned their loss while considering an appropriate response to the violence. Five widows grieved the loss of the men they loved.

The men left behind their wives and children, but their violent end did not negate the reason they had gone to Ecuador. Through a miracle of patient, prayerful, persistent faith in God, Elisabeth Elliot and Rachel Saint, Nate's sister, continued to reach out to the Waodani tribe and eventually bridged the gap between the two cultures.

On October 8, 1958, Elisabeth Elliot and her daughter, Valerie, then three and a half, entered the Waodani village and were welcomed and embraced by the very people who had killed the five missionaries. The thought of revenge never crossed Elisabeth's mind, even when she met Mincaye, the man who had murdered her husband. Without vengeance, she forgave him and continued the original mission of introducing the Waodani tribe to God.

In 1958, there were six hundred Waodani living in Ecuador. Today, the tribe has grown to nearly two thousand. The murder rate of fifty years ago has dropped to only ten or twenty killings per year. A culture that once stood on the brink of extinction has been transformed into a culture of life.

There are two reasons for that change. First, Elisabeth Elliot lived with the Waodani, modeled a better way of life, and introduced them to God. Second, she didn't do it alone. Rachel Saint also lived with the Waodani (in fact, for more than three decades), and she and others helped to translate the Bible into the Waodani language.

Today, Steve Saint, Rachel's nephew and Nate's son, continues the work by meeting the medical and dental needs of the people. Mincaye, the man who murdered his father, is his main advocate. Now in his seventies, Mincaye says, "We acted badly until they brought God's carvings [the Bible]. Now we walk his trail. In our place, whoever has fever, cut, hurting, they come to us because they know we care. We take care of their hurt, then we teach them how to take care of their heart. I teach them God's carvings."[5]

Elisabeth Elliot and others like her who have devoted their lives to spreading the love of God, despite painful and costly circumstances, are what I would call modern-day saints. They give no thought to themselves, but only to serving God and his people wherever they are found.

Bob Dylan says, "A saint is a person who gives of himself totally and freely, without strings. He is neither deaf nor blind. And yet he's both."[6] Elisabeth Elliot and the others were neither deaf nor blind to the hostile world they entered, and yet they were deaf and blind to the hatred and violence they encountered.

They were deaf and blind to revenge.

They were not deaf and blind to the love they gave in response. ✓

Elizabeth Dole has pursued a life of faith in God and was placed at the top of the world for all to see, applaud, respect, and envy. Elisabeth Elliot pursued a life of faith in God and lost her husband at the hand of a murderer on the underside of the globe. How is it that they both claim the same unwavering commitment to God? It is easy to identify with Elizabeth Dole's reasoning, but what is it for Elisabeth Elliot? In her own words, "Next to the Incarnation, I know of no more staggering truth than that a sovereign God has ordained my participation."[7]

Jim and Elisabeth Elliot, ordinary college students, went to another part of the world and made a profound impact on people's lives. It's a story fifty years in the making of how a group of young people, with persevering faith and the support of others who were willing to serve and sacrifice, was able to transform an entire culture.

Your destiny will not take place in a vacuum; it will require the participation of others. On occasion, God will give you a gentle nudge to remind you that he is with you.

ACTIONS

Write down your answers to the following questions:

What do you want others to say about you after you're gone?

What are the three most important things in your life?

What is at least one thing for which you are willing to die?

COMPLETED BY GOD

FULFILLING YOUR DESTINY

*What does it profit a man if he gains
the whole world, yet loses his soul?*

—JESUS OF NAZARETH

LAST EVENING, I left off writing and returned home, troubled and disturbed. It was time to write the next chapter, and I thought I had the essential stories I wanted to share, but I was unsettled.

What was I missing?

Still questioning, I drove home, put on my winter coat, and went out to shovel snow from the driveway. I heard geese in the distance and was reminded of a promise God made to me several years ago. He told me that he was the author of life and the giver of gifts, and that one of his gifts to me, as a reminder of his continual presence, was geese in flight. Now, every time I see geese in formation or hear their honking flight, they remind me that God is with me.

With snow falling, and the cloud ceiling at no more than 120 feet, I couldn't see anything overhead. The sound of the honking faded into the distance and then returned, growing louder until a V-formation of geese swept down from the clouds and flew directly over my head before disappearing into the distance.

I smiled and said, "Thank you, God." I knew he was there and that he wanted to speak to me. He was nudging me to look more deeply into my experience. When I did, he told me that I would discover and fulfill my destiny through my weakness.

Somehow, we become more useful in God's hands when we let him reveal himself through our weaknesses. When we entrust our weaknesses to God, he makes the ordinary extraordinary. I'm vividly reminded of this whenever I think of Viktor Frankl. ✓

Viktor Frankl was a Holocaust survivor of four Nazi death camps that took the lives of his wife, father, mother, and brother. His experience at Auschwitz and the other concentration camps left him in the balance between life and death. During his internment, he daily questioned the purpose of existence and the value of the individual soul. He was extremely aware of how infinitely small, weak, imperfect, and destitute he was.

One day, on a march toward an unknown destination and possibly death, he was confronted with a thought:

> For the first time in my life I saw the truth as it is set into song by so many poets, proclaimed as the final wisdom by so many thinkers. The truth—that love is the ultimate and the highest goal to which men can aspire. Then I

grasped the meaning of the greatest secret that human poetry and human thought and belief have to impart: *the salvation of man is through love and in love. . . .* For the first time in my life, I was able to understand the meaning of the words, "The angels are lost in perpetual contemplation of an infinite glory."[1]

Viktor Frankl was able only to take the next step toward an unknown destination when truth broke into his world. This happened at a point of utter weakness, when his life was in the hands of a vicious captor.

God uses our weaknesses so that we will open the doors of our hearts to know and understand him. He takes all that we give of ourselves, including our frailties, failures, and shortcomings, and creates something beautiful out of them. Frankl became a world-renowned psychotherapist.

The Bible says,

> Think of what you were when you were called. Not many of you were wise by human standards; not many were influential; not many were of noble birth. But God chose the foolish things of the world to shame the wise; God chose the weak things of the world to shame the strong. He chose the lowly things of this world and the despised things—and the things that are not—to nullify the things that are, so that no one may boast before him. (1 Corinthians 1:26-29)

Is your destiny discovered through your weakness? Is it fulfilled in love? Many others besides Elisabeth Elliot and Viktor Frankl have traveled the road of weakness and have met God along the way.✓

Dr. Paul Brand died on July 2, 2003, following a lifetime of medical service, particularly to those afflicted with leprosy in third-world countries. Author Philip Yancey traveled with him on occasion and recorded the following:

> I remember visiting Sadan, one of Dr. Paul Brand's former leprosy patients, in India. He looked like a miniature version of Gandhi: skinny, bald, perched cross-legged on the edge of a bed. In a high-pitched, singsong voice, he told me wrenching stories of past rejection: the classmates who tormented him in school, the driver who kicked him—literally, with his shoe—off a public bus, the many employers who refused to hire him despite his training and talent, the hospitals that turned him away out of unwarranted fear.
>
> Sadan then recounted the elaborate sequence of medical procedures—tendon transfers, nerve strippings, toe amputations, and cataract removal—performed by Dr. Brand and his ophthalmologist wife. He spoke for half an hour, recounting a life that was a catalogue of human suffering. But as we sipped our last cup of tea in his home, Sadan made this astonishing statement: "Still, I must say that I am now happy that I had this disease."
>
> "Happy?" I asked, incredulous.
>
> "Yes," replied Sadan. "Apart from leprosy, I would have been a normal man with a normal family, chasing wealth and a higher position in society. I would never have known such wonderful people as Dr. Paul and Dr.

Margaret, and I would never have known the God who lives in them."[2]

I admit that I never want to walk the path that Sadan has traveled, but I want to reflect shalom, the "total well-being" that characterizes his life. Through his leprosy, he found meaning in his life.

Have you ever thought that God might want to use you to help another person discover his or her destiny? Have you ever thought that the God who lives within you, as he did in Paul and Margaret, is what you have to offer to the world? God in his grace reaches down to us in the circumstances of our lives, touching us with the joy and tragedy that open the door to our destiny. C. S. Lewis speaks of this through the image of a house being remodeled:

> Imagine yourself as a living house. God comes in to rebuild that house. At first, perhaps, you can understand what he is doing. He is getting the drains right and stopping the leaks in the roof and so on. You knew the jobs needed doing and so you are not surprised. But presently, he starts knocking the house about in a way that hurts abominably and does not seem to make sense. What on earth is he up to? The explanation is that he is building quite a different house from the one you thought of—throwing out a new wing here, putting on an extra floor there, running up towers, making courtyards. You thought you were going to be made into a decent little cottage, but he is building a palace. He intends to come and live in it himself.[3]

Often it's by knocking down walls that God is able to make us into the house—or palace—that we were destined to be. ✓

Your destiny will also come as the result of a journey. Our destiny includes both the destination (God) and the journey (the process of reaching him). In knowing our destination, we gain hope and strength. In knowing our final fate (becoming like him), the journey is given its meaning (its purpose for today). As we make the journey in a meaningful way (by serving others), the destination is brought into clearer focus (a vision of what is to come).

It is my destiny to know and love God, serve others, and some day be present with God. When I am present with him, I will become as he is. I will be transformed into a far better reflection of him than I am today. Because of this, today is important, I am important, and others are important. Where I am going gives value to the process of getting there. My todays create my tomorrow, and my actions are an integral part of my destination.

Elisabeth Elliot, Rachel Saint, and Steve Saint spent their days in primitive conditions with primitive people, ever mindful of their violent ways. Their work was vibrantly meaningful because the Waodani people were of value to them. They experienced great losses, yet they continued to reach out in love. They lived with the end in mind and were confident they could put their trust in God, regardless of the trials they faced. Elisabeth Elliot said, "Every experience of trial puts us to this test: 'Do you trust God or don't you?'"[4]

I have often clung to these words from Psalm 73:23-24: "You hold me by my right hand. You guide me with your counsel, and afterward you will take me into glory." God is with me to hold, protect, and guide me. Only "afterward" will I enter into glory with him.

There's a connection between my journey and my destination, and both are valuable. They are different ends of the same string, different parts of the same story, and different seasons of the same life. When I become discouraged during this particular season of life, I find ways to obtain comfort and a clear perspective. God is accomplishing his purposes through me on this journey. As the author of the book of Romans says,

> I consider that our present sufferings are not worth comparing with the glory that will be revealed in us. . . . The Spirit helps us in our weakness. . . . And we know that in all things God works for the good of those who love him, who have been called according to his purpose.
>
> . . . Who shall separate us from the love of Christ? Shall trouble or hardship or persecution or famine or nakedness or danger or sword?
>
> . . . For I am convinced that neither death nor life, neither angels nor demons, neither the present nor the future, nor any powers, neither height nor depth, nor anything else in all creation, will be able to separate us from the love of God. (Romans 8:18, 26, 28, 35, 38-39)

These verses tell us what to expect from life, what we and others may go through. We will face life and death, angels and demons, and all sorts of opposition within creation, but nothing will ever separate us from God.

If that is the case, then how we live the journey surely matters. Thomas à Kempis underscores this point very well: "My child, what you do, do well. Work faithfully in my vineyard. I will reward you. Peace will come on a day which is known to the Lord, and then there shall be no day or night as at present, but perpetual light, infinite brightness, lasting peace, and safe repose. Then death will be banished, and there will be health unfailing.

There will be no anxiety then, but blessed joy and sweet, noble companionship."[5]

How you live today can bring that reality one step closer.

The smallest act of obedience in your life can be the seed of a miracle in someone else's life. The five men who gave up their lives on a sandbar in the jungles of Ecuador chose not to use their weapons. Someone who knew them well said that they did not use their guns because they were prepared to meet God in heaven. Their act of obedience was the raw material of a miracle that continues fifty years later. ✓

REFLECTIONS

As God's chosen child, you are also a child of destiny. Ecclesiastes 3:11 says that God has "set eternity in the hearts of men."

What does that mean to you?

What is your destiny?

What makes your life worth living?

What will you do today to make a difference in your world?

CAN YOU HEAR ME NOW?

LISTENING FOR GOD'S CALL

What you are called to do is already within you.
God wants you to carry his dream as
a pregnant woman carries her child.

—DR. MYLES MUNROE

ON APRIL 20, 1999, shots rang out and pipe bombs exploded at Columbine High School in Littleton, Colorado. Eric Harris, age eighteen, and Dylan Klebold, seventeen, wearing black trench coats and laughing at their helpless victims and fleeing targets, murdered one teacher and twelve students, and maimed or wounded twenty-three others.

With their rampage, Harris and Klebold were "celebrating" Adolf Hitler's 110th birthday, and they intended to touch off a chain reaction of hatred and chaos. One of their specific targets was a girl named Rachel Scott, whom they wanted to kill because of her faith in God. ✓

Just hours before her final breath, Rachel made a prophetic entry in the journal she carried in her backpack. On the cover, where she had written, "I won't be labeled as average," the words were pierced by a bullet. She had also written, "I write, not for the sake of glory, not for the sake of fame, not for the sake of success, but for the sake of my soul—Rachel Joy."[1]

The last entry in Rachel's diary was a drawing of her eyes and a stream of thirteen tears watering a rose. Her tears, upon touching the rose, appeared to turn into drops of blood. The number thirteen seems prophetic: Thirteen people died the day she drew the picture.

Rachel's father later discovered another drawing from one year earlier that showed a rose growing out of a columbine plant, the Colorado state flower for which the high school was named. The drawing included a cross inscribed with the words, "Greater love has no man than this, that a man would lay down his life for his friends!" ✓

Eric Harris and Dylan Klebold had put in place some ninety-five explosive devices, "enough firepower to wipe out their school and potentially hundreds of students. They had assembled and planted forty-eight carbon dioxide bombs, or 'crickets,' twenty-seven pipe bombs, eleven 1.5-gallon propane containers, seven incendiary devices with forty-plus gallons of flammable liquid, and two duffel bag bombs with twenty-pound liquefied-petroleum gas tanks."[2]

We know that their cars, their homes, and their own bodies were wired with explosives. Their arsenal of deadly weapons had been strategically planted at crucial population centers throughout the school to ensure the greatest human destruction. Had the large bombs planted in the cafeteria detonated, they would have sucked all the air out of the room, suffocating whatever students and teachers were not killed by the explosions. ✓

❧

Richard Castaldo, Rachel's friend, was eating lunch with her outside the school library when Harris and Klebold approached them and opened fire without provocation. Richard was paralyzed from multiple gunshot wounds, and Rachel's legs and chest were severely wounded. Harris and Klebold then walked away.

Moments later, they returned. Eric Harris grabbed Rachel by her hair, pulled her head up, and asked, "Do you believe in God?"

Rachel responded, "You know I do."

Harris said, "Then go be with him!" as he shot her in the head.

God's little child was violently returned to him, but not before her young life had planted many seeds of love and kindness.

In the end, the two young perpetrators committed suicide.

It was remarkable that most of the explosives they had built and planted were never detonated. It was a miracle that many more were not killed. ✓

❧

Rachel seemed to know that she would make a difference in the world. She was aware of her coming fate, as indicated by a number of things she wrote in her journals. She sensed that she would never reach twenty and would never marry. "This may be my last year," she wrote. "I have gotten what I can." She quoted a phrase from a song: "Just passing by, just coming thru, not staying long, I always knew, this home I have, will never last."

Rachel's journal entries, including many of her prayers to God, suggest that she listened for her calling in the world. "I want to reach a new level with you, God," she wrote. "Take me there."

In the aftermath of the Columbine tragedy, many things appeared to be more than unexplained coincidences. In their videotaped statement, the shooters said, "We need to . . . kick-start a revolution. We need to get a chain reaction going here!"

Ironically, in the days before the shootings, Rachel wrote, "I have this theory that if one person can go out of their way to show compassion, then it will start a chain reaction of the same."

Rachel Scott was called to make a difference, and she listened to that voice. She was an ordinary person who left an extraordinary legacy. ✓

I met Rachel's parents, sister, and brother at a Columbine memorial service in Littleton a year after the shootings. It was televised internationally and featured such notables as Governor Bill Owens and musical artist Michael W. Smith. I was there to host a televised satellite call-in broadcast called *America's Voice.* I was joined on the set by youth culture expert Josh McDowell and Rachel's father, Darrell Scott.

One man phoned in to challenge us by asking, "Why are you still talking about the killings? Why would you want to remember something so violent?"

Darrell replied, "This program is not intended to glorify the tragedy but to remember the lives that were lost, so we can embrace a future that can be made better through their loss. Their deaths have caused a lot of good to happen."

Darrell then told the story of a young boy, Austin Wiggins. Rachel helped him by holding an umbrella over his head while he changed his tire in the pouring rain. They had not met before. At Rachel's funeral, Austin tearfully introduced himself to Darrell and told how Rachel had befriended him. He had initially been rude and unreceptive to the kindness of this stranger, but he came to believe that he had been visited by an angel on that very gloomy day. The kind, simple act of holding an umbrella in the rain began a chain reaction in Austin Wiggins's life.

Darrell mentioned an occasion when he was speaking at another high school. A young man told him that he had come to make fun of Rachel's death. He was also planning to blow up his school and kill his fellow students. Instead, he found Darrell's story of forgiveness in Rachel's memory so powerful that it brought about a remarkable change of heart, and he abandoned his terrorist plans. A year later, the life of one ordinary girl, Rachel Joy Scott, was still making a powerful difference in the world.

As our broadcast came to a close, Darrell said that Columbine was a wake-up call for America. America's youth have been stripped of their spiritual heritage and are searching for far more than their parents, educators, politicians, or business leaders are providing. In the twelve months following the shootings, Darrell, his family, and other families touched by Columbine saw thousands of people's lives changed as they told the story of hope contained within the tragedy.

There was a chain reaction of love and forgiveness.

Rachel lived for just seventeen years, and her life and death have touched millions of people around the world through the testimony of her family and her journals. She answered a call, and despite her human failings, God used her to change the world. ✓

∾

"Calling" can be defined in various ways. "A religious vocation regarded as divinely inspired" seems to apply to clergy who are called to serve God vocationally. Another definition speaks of being summoned to a specific duty, with an inner urging toward a certain action. Whether from above or from within . . . there is an inner urging towards a passion, a cause or a career.

Let me suggest another definition of "calling."

I believe we each have a divine destiny, a "call" that is an invitation from God to do a specific task for him. I believe that God has a purpose for our lives. The question is whether we will seek and listen for his call. I believe that God is continually speaking to us—it's just a matter of our learning to recognize his voice.

How do you seek his call in your life?

There isn't any simple formula. God communicates with each of us in distinctive ways to which we are uniquely designed to respond. However, we can open ourselves to God's call and make ourselves receptive to our destiny.

It is easier to hear the whispered, still, small voice of God when we reduce the noise level in our lives. My phone, fax, e-mail, wife, daughters, boss, family, friends, employees, board, and community commitments; radio, TV, cable networks, satellite technology, political pundits, poverty, movies, natural disasters, the Internet, news of the day, thoughts of past failures, anxiety about the future, and even my church all compete for my attention on a daily basis.

Either they have something I want, or I have something they want.

Like you, I'm confronted daily by men and women with straight teeth, beautiful smiles, and perfect skin asking me to buy something, invest in something, or believe the latest gossip about someone. Like you, I'm disturbed by the arrogance of political leaders who communicate in sound bites for the primary purpose of perpetuating the power of their political parties. It is difficult to remain focused on meaningful issues when we are besieged by so many competing and contradictory voices.

In our Western world, where even the "have nots" have more than ever before and where the "haves" live in crowded affluence, we lack the peace that would seem to be within our grasp because one more voice is always calling out to us.

If we are to hear God's voice, we have to eliminate unnecessary voices and the noise they create in our lives. We have to create silent spaces in our lives so that we can actively listen for God's voice. Have you created enough silent space to hear God?

What is your call? What difference will you make with your life today? ✓

REFLECTIONS

What do you find most extraordinary about Rachel Scott?

What "chain reaction" do you most want to start?

What is your calling?

THE STILL, SMALL VOICE

DISCERNING GOD'S INTENTIONS

*God, if I can't die then please
show me how to live.*

—JONI EARECKSON TADA

IN *Celebration of Discipline,* Richard Foster encourages us to position ourselves to hear and understand God's voice and to respond to his call: "If we hope to move beyond the superficialities of our culture we must be willing to go down into the recreating silences. There are vast unexplored inner regions that are just as real as the physical world. There is a call to join in the adventure, to be pioneers in this frontier of the spirit."[1]

We often fail to hear God's call because we're not listening, or because it is drowned out by the many competing voices in our world.

This noise is often intentionally sought out.

Mother Teresa believed that the greatest disease facing mankind is loneliness. We are lonely because we don't seek God, but instead we fill our lives with other things. When they occupy our attention, there is no room left for God to place something in our hands or in our hearts.

∞

May I suggest that you examine your life and evaluate the voices crying out for your attention?

What is really important?

Can you eliminate superficial noise?

Can you create the spiritual space to listen for his call?

I have found it very helpful to take a retreat from daily life now and then, just an hour or a day away from the rat race in a quiet place and time set apart for listening.

Years ago, I left my apartment in Denver to take advantage of a day alone with God in a cabin in the foothills of the Rockies. The morning did not begin as I expected. With Bible in hand and pad and pen by my side, I was dozing off within minutes. Angered (always a good thing to be when spending time with God), I stiffened my resolve to "push through" and I failed. I laid it all aside and took a nap. I woke, only to fight every thought, daydream, and distraction conceivable. When I failed again, I took refuge in a second nap. Upon later reflection, I realized that this was exactly what I needed to clear my mind and calm my spirit.

On my third try, I began to journal my thoughts and prayers about what God was telling me. The day that began with such a difficult struggle would become the genesis of what I am writing about in this book. I still have those notes.

God has been reshaping and maturing these thoughts over the past twenty-five years. God spoke to me, and I would never have heard his voice had I not gotten away from the bustle and noise to devote spiritual space to listening to him. ✓

∾

An old adage says that we can hear a great deal while listening to very little.

I turned on my cell phone recently after an early morning meeting and discovered a voice mail message that had been left the previous evening. I listened to the message, but I couldn't understand the garbled words. I moved to another part of the building for better reception, listened, and thought I heard the words "Air Force One." I was immediately intrigued and wanted to hear the rest of the message.

Moving outside helped, and on my third try, I understood the whole message: "Hi, Harvey. This is Air Force One. I have Mr. Towey wanting to speak to you, and he said to give him a call tomorrow at the White House office." Jim Towey is the former director of the White House Office of Faith-Based and Community Initiatives. I had contacted him with a request for President Bush to speak at a community-wide leadership event. Jim was flying to Washington, D.C., with the president on Air Force One and asked the plane operator to return my phone call. In retrieving his message, I fought through poor reception three times to hear his voice from the air.

We must really want to hear God's calling.

If the presence of God is of value to us, and we desire to hear his calling, we will seek him with the same determination and passion that I felt as I pursued the message from Air Force One. ✓

~

God's calling sometimes comes to us through our interactions with other people. My friend Jim Towey tells of the time that he met Mother Teresa.

In 1985, when he worked for U.S. Senator Mark Hatfield, Jim had an opportunity to visit Mother Teresa in India. By his own admission, he was interested in the trip for superficial reasons. He thought it would be "cool" to visit Mother Teresa, "get the tour, . . . drop a $20 on the table," and leave. To top it off, the return trip included five days in Hawaii! He certainly "didn't want to be around poor people."[2]

So he went on this junket.

Once there, the experience of being in Mother Teresa's presence and living in her world overwhelmed him. At one hospital, he was given cotton swabs and a bottle of antiseptic as the nurse instructed him to "go clean the man with scabies in bed 46."[3]

That day forever changed his life.

Jim heard God's calling in the "distressing disguise" of the poor and the sick. He went to serve as a volunteer and then as legal counsel for Mother Teresa for twelve years, including one year as a live-in staff person in her home for people with AIDS in Washington, D.C.

We often hear the whisper of God's calling in our contacts with other people. ✓

I'm learning to pay attention to fleeting thoughts and sudden impulses in my life. I think that God often gets our attention in this way. He is saying, "Hey, over here, I have something to tell you."

Many years ago, I was returning from a weekend with rancher friends in Limon, Colorado, after a great experience of getting good old-fashioned dirty, sweaty, and dog-tired while working with their livestock. The weekend included roping, injecting antibiotics into the steers, and branding, which I always find unnerving.

Right before leaving, I had a sense that God wanted my attention. A nudge or an urge to listen darted through my mind, so I paid attention to that as I silently drove the ninety miles back to Denver.

Two words came into my mind. I didn't understand either one at the time, but they stuck with me all the way back to town and for days afterward, which is unusual for me. I'm the person who will meet you one minute, then turn to my wife the next to ask her to tell me your name . . . again.

The words were *Shekinah Jedidiah.*

Those words rattled around in my mind for days, and finally I went in search of their meaning. *Shekinah* is "the presence of God, or the glory of God dwelling in the midst of his people." It denotes the immediate presence of God. *Jedidiah* means "beloved of the Lord."

The presence of God. The beloved of the Lord.

Was this a message for me? Was God telling me that I was his beloved and that he was with me?

I believe so. I still have my written notes from that experience of twenty-five years ago: "Harvey, I am with you and you are my beloved." God has spoken to me in many other ways since then, but never again in this way. I pursued a thought that stayed in my mind and followed an impulse that somehow touched my soul. I heard God's voice in the midst of all the other noises of life. It was God's way of speaking to me. ✓

How will you hear God's calling in your life? My way may not be your way—God will find a way that is unique to you.

God calls ordinary men and women to make a difference in their world in many different ways. It may be through whispers or impulses, visions or dreams. God speaks through nature, his Spirit, the counsel of godly friends, the body of Christ, and the circumstances of our lives.

God also speaks to us through the Bible, which reveals how God called other ordinary people to change their worlds and do his work. God appeared to Abraham and John in visions, sent an angel to the shepherds at Jesus' birth, visited Jacob in dreams, and spoke to Moses through the miracle of a burning bush.

I like Henry Blackaby's words on this subject. In his book *Experiencing God,* he identifies the means by which people heard God in the Old Testament:

> When God spoke, it was usually unique to the individual.
> When God spoke, the person was sure God was speaking.
> When God spoke, the person knew what God said.
> When God spoke, that was the encounter with God.[4]

God's call to you will be personal and individual.

It will be for your ears only, for your life only. It will be in words and language that you will intuitively understand. If, as with the words *Shekinah Jedidiah* for me, you hear words that you don't immediately understand, you will still recognize that they are for you, and that you can learn what God is communicating to you.

Most importantly, when you hear God's call to become more than ordinary, you will hear God saying, "You are my beloved, and I have a divine destiny for you." ✓

∾

So what is God calling you *to?*

The specifics of your call will be between you and God, and they will be unique to your relationship with him. Several characteristics are typical of God's calling to all of us, however. They change our ordinary lives, and we accomplish remarkable things.

GOD CALLS YOU TO BECOME MORE FULLY YOURSELF.

How do you become "fully yourself"?

We can't do this for ourselves—it is a process of allowing God to live more fully through us. He is our creator, and we are his creation. What better resource could we have as we make our unique journeys through life than to seek the one who designed us? We fail when we think that we should be just the way everyone else wants us to be. We fail when we try to live like everyone else and seek to duplicate the successes of our father, mother, brother, sister, mentor, hero, or boss.

The rabbi Zusya once said,
> "In the world to come I shall not be asked:
> 'Why were you not Moses?'
> I shall be asked:
> 'Why were you not Zusya?'"[5]

This truth was driven home to me a number of years ago. I struggled as my contemporaries in college went to graduate school to become psychiatrists and clinical psychologists. I felt that anything short of such lofty goals represented failure.

In the midst of this struggle, God gave me a liberating thought: *Harvey, you've proven that you can be like everyone else (dean's list, major university, success); now it's time to prove that you can be yourself.*

When I stopped pursuing the path of my peers, I found my path, and that frees me to express my heart, my soul, and my real interests. It led me to the inner cities of Denver and Columbus, to the prisons of Colorado and Ohio, to the Ohio statehouse and the White House, and to the small villages of Cielo and Nazaret in the Dominican Republic.

I would do it all again!

∾

As a father, I am most fully pleased when my children are each free to express their unique personalities, gifts, and abilities. When they do that, they shine; and when they shine, I shine!

This is how God feels about you.

If you're like me, you aren't always satisfied with yourself and your performance. We look at our shortcomings, consider our weaknesses, and compare our strengths to those of others.

I sometimes wonder how my exceedingly common life can possibly count.

In those moments, I turn to Psalm 103:3-5: It is the Lord "who forgives all your sins and heals all your diseases, who redeems your life from the pit and crowns you with love and compassion, who satisfies your desires with good things so that your youth is renewed like the eagle's." I love that! ✓

GOD CALLS YOU TO DEVELOP YOUR CHARACTER.

When you are free to be fully yourself, you give yourself permission to be who you really are. When you choose a path in life that leads you to become a better person, you give God permission to develop your character.

My life path took me away from the quiet, plush, carpeted office of a clinical psychologist to the steel-reinforced windows and razor-wire fences of prisons; the litter-strewn alleys of unsafe neighborhoods; and occasionally, to an encounter with a violent teen or angry adult. It put me and my family in harm's way and pushed me outside of my comfort zone. I had to discover and develop resources that I did not know were within me. Each new experience built upon previous encounters and expanded my life. Each new obstacle forced me to grow. Each unwelcome interruption added a new brick of fortitude to my character that better prepared me for the road ahead.

These cumulative experiences have equipped me for the assignments I have been given in life. Pain and setbacks are requirements if I am to mature as a person. They develop essential qualities of moral strength and insight that I need to succeed in the tasks God has put before me.

From being an uncomfortable, questioning follower, I have

grown into being a leader and a teacher. I have often thought that others were far better suited to my assignment than I am, but I have become a model for others to follow.

I believe that Army infantryman Audie Murphy is a perfect example of this. When he leaped to the top of the burning tank destroyer and turned the .50-caliber machine gun to face the overwhelming number of approaching enemy troops, he had never faced a situation quite like it before. Still, he drew upon his fight to survive during the Great Depression, the hours he'd spent hunting wild game to provide food for his family, and his prior combat experience to create his extraordinary success in that life-defining hour. ✓

GOD CALLS YOU TO REDEMPTIVE ACTION.

One definition of the word *redemption* is "setting another free by paying a ransom." It is other-centered—an urge to seek another's well-being at a cost to yourself. This impulse can be transformed into meaningful, purposeful action that reveals your true identity and the principles you believe in most deeply.

What you do is a reflection of who you are, so you "do what you are" rather than "being what you do." Thomas Merton writes, "My soul does not find itself unless it acts." To complete my thought, I would say, "My soul does not find itself unless it acts for the well-being of my fellow man or woman."[6]

That's what turns action into redemptive action.

That's what Rachel Scott and Audie Murphy knew so very well. Audie was the only one behind the machine gun, and Rachel wrote on a cross inside her journal, "Greater love has no man than this, that a man would lay down his life for his friends!"

It's one thing to say that we believe in something, and quite another to do something about it. I sometimes need this reminder from the Bible: "Faith by itself, if it is not accompanied by action, is dead" (James 2:17).

If we live only in the activities of our lives and their measurable results—promotion, corner office, sales goals, country club membership—we tend to remain alienated from others.

The person who does not believe in God must act to prove his worth.

The person who knows God acts out of his or her relationship with God.

When we act from the center of our authentic selves, we are brought into intimacy with others. Action never creates its own significance or value. Redemptive action always flows from a relationship with God and values the life of another.

So what is the value of a common, ordinary life?

What is the value of *your* life?

Albert Einstein writes, "The universe could not operate on chance. God does not play dice."[7] If this is true, you are not a die rolled across the gambling table of life by a distant, indifferent, higher life form. You were created intentionally and marked for a purpose that is revealed through your redemptive actions.

What makes an ordinary person extraordinary?

Ordinary people become extraordinary when they respond to God's call, give themselves permission to become fully themselves, give God permission to mold their character, and take redemptive action in their public and private lives.

Someone once said, "A call is a conviction that steadily deepens when faced with the facts of the case, so that sooner or later it becomes a matter of obedience or disobedience."

What is God calling *you* to do? ✓

ACTIONS

Schedule a time in your calendar (write it down) to "get away from it all" for four hours. Make sure the location will provide uninterrupted time to reflect, listen, and journal your thoughts.

During your time away, write down what you hear. Write down what you think your calling is.

Write down one practical way in which you can act on your calling. Tell one other person what you're going to do. Go and do it.

BELIEVING IS SEEING

ENVISIONING YOUR FUTURE

It would be no surprise if a study of secret causes were undertaken to find that every golden era in human history proceeds from the devotion and righteous passion of some single individual. This does not set aside the sovereignty of God; it simply indicates the instrument through which he uniformly works. There are no bona fide mass movements; it just looks that way. At the center of the column there is always one man who knows his God and knows where he is going.

—RICHARD ELLSWORTH DAY

WHAT IS *vision?*

This word is tossed around in everyday conversations, but its meaning is difficult to grasp with a single definition. We know that leaders are supposed to have it, that without it people perish, and that God sometimes uses it to communicate his desires.

Vision can be defined as

A mental image.

An imaginative contemplation.

Something perceived in a dream.

Something supernaturally revealed, as to a prophet.

The ability to perceive something not actually visible.

Something seen by other-than-normal sight.

There are other definitions. Matthew Kelly states, "Vision is God's dream for you."[1] Laura Fortgang says, "Vision is a compelling image of an achievable future."[2] Chuck Swindoll writes, "Vision is the ability to see God's presence, to perceive God's power, to focus on God's plan in spite of the obstacles."[3]

What is a visionary? *Visionary* is often defined as

Existing only in the mind; not real; imaginary.

Not capable of being put into effect.

Not realistic; impractical.

Characterized by impractical ideas or schemes.

A person whose ideas or plans are impractical, too idealistic or fantastic; a dreamer.

Do you have vision? Are you a visionary?

I define a visionary as one who has the ability to see what is not yet as if it were already present. Visionaries have the ability to see around the bend in the road. I believe that kind of vision is available to everyone. ✓

VISIONARY PEOPLE KNOW GOD AND KNOW WHERE THEY ARE GOING.

Visionaries are often met with skepticism because they see beyond the commonplace to what could be and, on many occasions, to what will be. Inherent in such vision is a call to change what *is* in order to fulfill what is to come. Vision precedes change, and change is usually met with opposition. If you want to pursue a vision in your life, you must know that it will be opposed—and you must be prepared for this.

Dr. Myles Munroe, chairman of the International Third World Leaders Association and a United Nations non-governmental delegate, introduced me to some deeper insights on this topic on one of his trips to Columbus to address the Columbus Leadership Prayer Breakfast. During one of our conversations, he said, "Vision is a glimpse of our purpose. If a vision is from God, it will require God to be accomplished. If it is God's dream, he will pay for it. Therefore, find something to do that makes you afraid every morning. Pursue a vision for your life that requires God's intervention to be fully accomplished. Imitate God; he made you. Every vision will be tested for authenticity, so expect problems and obstacles."[4]

In other words, if it's God's vision, it is worth pursuing.

It cannot fail, even if we fail in some ways as we go along.

I believe that God has a vision for you that will honor your gifts, personality, and call. Are you prepared? Are you pursuing a vision of what will be?

What do I mean by the chapter title "Believing Is Seeing"? If we seek God by pursuing his vision for our lives, we must move beyond the limitations of any dictionary definition. We must trust him enough to begin to see his vision for our work in the world.

The biblical story of Lazarus is found in John 11. When Lazarus became sick, his sisters Mary and Martha sent word of his illness to Jesus, yet Jesus remained where he was for two more days. Lazarus died and was buried. Upon Jesus' arrival, Martha said, "If you had been here, my brother would not have died." Jesus was moved by the loss of this loved one, and he wept, but in God's plan, the death of Lazarus led to his resurrection, as Jesus brought him back to life.

Jesus said to Martha, "He who believes in me will live, even though he dies; and whoever lives and believes in me will never die. Do you believe this?"

"Yes, Lord," she told him. "I believe."

As the stone was being rolled away from the tomb, Jesus said, "Did I not tell you that if you believed, you would see the glory of God?"[5]

That's it, right there!

When we believe God, we begin to see what he wants us to see. Seeing isn't believing, because many at the tomb that day saw the miracle but did not believe in God. Those who believed saw God's glory revealed in the miracle. Belief and vision go hand in hand, because "believing is seeing."

As we draw closer to God, our view of ourselves, others, and the world will become clearer. God has granted us the ability to see beyond the vision of our eyes, the understanding of our minds, and the desires of our hearts so that we can embrace the future that he created us to fulfill.

Our vision defines us. Our vision of God shapes us.

Sometimes our vision is clear and gives us definition, direction, and meaning. Sometimes our vision has cloudy edges that are not fully developed and seem to stretch us impossibly. Don't be distracted by the lack of clarity that so often comes at the beginning of vision; it will come. Sometimes, having our "vision" clarified will happen in more than one stage as well, like the time Jesus healed a blind man but restored the man's sight in two separate phases:

> They came to Bethsaida, and some people brought a blind man and begged Jesus to touch him. He took the blind man by the hand and led him outside the village. When he had spit on the man's eyes and put his hands on him, Jesus asked, "Do you see anything?"
>
> He looked up and said, "I see people; they look like trees walking around."
>
> Once more Jesus put his hands on the man's eyes. Then his eyes were opened, his sight was restored, and he saw everything clearly. (Mark 8:22-25)

What does vision do?

- Vision enables us to focus on what is not yet as if it were already present.

- Vision gives us an image of the future that frees us from the distracting and competing demands of life.

- Vision helps us to focus on an achievable end that is fulfilled in service to others.

David Steward understands this as well as anyone I know.

My first conversation with David gave me some insight into his remarkable multi-billion-dollar business success. I had a telephone appointment with him, but when I phoned, he was unavailable for our scheduled conversation. I dialed his assistant and learned that his earlier appointment in downtown St. Louis had run long and that he would call me back during his return trip to his office. When he called, the first thing he did was to apologize for missing our appointment. He told me that "people and punctuality are priorities" and expressed his regrets for missing my call.

That's rare. For the chairman of any company, let alone a multi-billion-dollar corporation, to apologize to an unknown person calling from 450 miles away for a first-time phone conversation on a busy work day is a rare character quality.

You may ask, "Being courteous comes from having a vision?" The answer is yes, especially if it's a vision that finds its fulfillment in serving others.

David Steward is the founder of World Wide Technology, a company he started in 1990 with four employees and four thousand square feet of office space to distribute computer hardware, software, and IT services to the federal government. Today, WWT and its affiliate company, Telcobuy.com, with headquarters in St. Louis, Missouri, are the leading electronic procurement and logistics companies in the information technology and telecommunications industries. The number of employees has increased to more than one thousand, and the four thousand square feet of office space is now a million-plus square-foot facility. Their annual revenue is nearly $3 billion. It all began with a vision that focused on the "not yet as if it already were."

David grew up in Clinton, Missouri, in a world often defined by race, poverty, alienation, and fear. Those characteristics defined the world around David's family, but not the world of the Steward family. David's older brothers and sisters went to Lincoln, an all-black school with only two teachers for grades one through twelve. Their school supplies were hand-me-down books left over from the white school on the better side of the tracks. The dilapidated school was a world away from the privileged educational resources available to whites.

David says, "How we lived was quite a contrast to the lifestyle of the white kids. Even so, my mother kept telling us that we should never resent anyone who had more than we had. Again and again, she said, 'You can do anything you set your heart to, son, and someday you'll have all those nice things too.' Instead of being limited by my depressing circumstances, I looked beyond the confines of my small hometown and focused on my vision of what God had in store for me. When I started out, I knew the road would be bumpy and filled with obstacles."[6]

David attended Franklin Elementary School, where he was the only African-American boy in his class. He lived with educational racism and social racism in the form of separate-but-equal community resources. He now experiences the occasional "marketplace racism" that stereotypes African-Americans as incompetent to lead in the world of information technology. Still, David had a vision to serve others through the world of information technology and to build a billion-dollar company in the process. He has achieved that goal. He now has a new vision to grow WWT into a $10 billion company.

How will this be achieved? In describing his vision, David said,

> A vision is a definite goal about what you want your company to be in the future. A vision isn't about what you want to do for you; it's about what you can do to better

serve people. When you have a vision to own a multibil-
lion-dollar company or become a multimillionaire, that
is simply wishful thinking, but when you have a vision
about how to benefit others—that's an entirely different
story.

When you fill a need for others, wealth follows.

That's the reward, not the vision.

I'm convinced that what our company sells more than
anything else is love and energy. Love and energy surface
when you have complete faith and confidence in God's
Word, when you fully believe in what he can do in your
life. You will have an abundance of success, but it's not
personal gratification you seek; instead, everything you do
is directed to the benefit of others.[7]

David Steward has built America's largest African-American
owned company, according to *Black Enterprise*. In May 2002,
he was recognized by *Ebony* as one of the "100 Most Influential
Black Americans." The company began with a vision to serve
others; it was fueled by diligent persistence, hard work, attention to detail, risk-taking, and faith in God. If ever there was a
company destined to reach $10 billion in annual revenue, this
is the one.

David's vision allowed him to maintain focus on an achievable
future that overcame racism and fear to accomplish far beyond
what anyone else in Clinton, Missouri, could believe or imagine—except, of course, his mom and dad.

His vision, the undercurrent of his faith in God, and the support of his parents and family kept him focused on his dream.
He refused to be dismayed by the opposition that came with the
color of his skin. When he began his business, he did not reach
immediate success. On one occasion, he ran out of his office

to retrieve a briefcase from a car that was being repossessed for non-payment. Though he went into debt and had bill collectors knocking at his door, he maintained his course because he believed that God had given him his vision and would support him.

Focusing on the "not yet" as if it already were allowed him to overcome the distractions and competing demands of many other opportunities and obstacles in life.

In the next chapter, we will consider some other characteristics of vision. ✓

REFLECTIONS

In your own words, what is vision?

What can having vision do for you?

STRENGTH AND STABILITY

KEEPING THE DREAM ALIVE

*Darest thou now, O soul, walk out with me
toward the unknown region, where neither
ground is for the feet nor any path to follow?*

—WALT WHITMAN

IN THE PREVIOUS CHAPTER, we considered the meaning of *vision* and *visionary,* and we started to look at what vision can accomplish in our lives. First, we realized that vision, like faith, enables us to think about things that haven't happened yet as though they were already concrete realities in the world. Now let's see what else vision will do for us. ✓

VISION MOTIVATES US TO TAKE
REDEMPTIVE ACTION IN THE WORLD.

Vision gives us an image of the future that generates a determined and meaningful course of action that is fulfilled by serving others.

In his book *Keeping the Dream Alive,* Robert Dale states, "Our dreams give us a basis for initiative and service. They provide launch pads for action, a toehold from which to begin work."[1] In other words, vision gives birth to passion. Passion inspires commitment and results in meaningful, determined action. Someone once said, "A vision and a task are the hope of the world." Our redemptive action creates a better future for all of creation.

Vision gives us a basis for action. What does it mean to pursue a determined and meaningful course of action? A woman who lived from 1820 to 1913 gives us some ideas. Should you or I ever come close to achieving what she did, we would be exceedingly blessed. Her name is Harriet Tubman.

Harriet was born Araminta Ross to parents Benjamin Ross and Harriet Greene near Cambridge on the eastern shore of Maryland. At age twelve, she suffered a serious blow to the head that gave her a lifelong battle with narcolepsy. Her childhood was filled with the harsh work of a field hand, little education, and the severe punishment that was common to slaves. She later adopted her mother's name, Harriet, as her own, and at age twenty-five she married John Tubman, a freeman.

In 1849, Harriet left her husband of five years, fearing that she would be sold to a slave owner in the Deep South. She escaped alone and traveled through Pennsylvania to Philadelphia, where she settled. Two years later, on a return journey to contact her husband, she discovered that he had taken a new wife.

With "I can only die but once" as her motto, she began the work that led to her being called "The Moses of Her People." In 1851, Harriet began relocating members of her family to St. Catharine's in Ontario, Canada, where she had her base of operations until 1857, when she rescued her aging parents from slavery. Over the next ten years, she made at least nineteen trips from the North into the South and rescued more than three hundred slaves.

By 1863, Harriet had the enormous sum of forty thousand dollars posted on her life, dead or alive, because of her work on the Underground Railroad. It is said that in all of her trips to free slaves, not a single life was lost. She was gone for weeks at a time, running daily risks while preparing for her passengers on the Underground Railroad. She was diminutive, had several front teeth missing, and wore a bandana on her head; she looked so much like so many other slaves that she blended in and was never captured.

She often went behind enemy lines to collect information on cotton warehouses, ammunition depots, and slaves waiting to be liberated. It was a life of stealth, danger, and possible death, and yet it was her determined course of action. Her vision is summed up in the following statements:

"I can't die but once."

"Mah people mus' go free."

"I always tole God, I'm gwine to hole stiddy on to You."

"You've got to see me trou."

Her strong faith in God, dedication to her fellow slaves, and her utter disregard for personal consequences fueled her passionate course of redemptive action.

> When going on these journeys she often lay alone in the forests all night. Her whole soul was filled with awe of the mysterious Unseen Presence, which thrilled her with such depths of emotion that all other care and fear vanished. Then she seemed to speak with her Maker "as a man talketh with his friend"; her child-like petitions had direct answers, and beautiful visions lifted her up above all doubt and anxiety into serene trust and faith. No man can be a hero without this faith in some form; the sense that he walks not in his own strength, but leaning on an almighty arm. Call it fate, destiny, what you will, Moses of old, Moses of today, believed it to be Almighty God."[2]

John Tubman lived the remainder of his life as a freeman. Harriet lived her life as a free person.

She sustained her vision by a deep faith in God and the desire to serve him and her fellow slaves. Miraculously, she survived all the miles, years, and each brush with death as God affirmed all that she did. At the end of the Civil War, she settled in Auburn, New York, married Nelson Davis, and became active in support of women's rights. In 1995, Harriet Tubman was honored by the federal government with a commemorative postage stamp.[3]

Harriet was motivated by a deep desire to help and serve others. Her motivation was revealed in her acts of setting others free from slavery. She had a vision of blacks walking free and living free. Though she hoped and prayed that others would find freedom as she had, she did not stop there. She did something about it. She put her freedom and her life on the line. ✓

VISION PROVIDES STRENGTH AND
STABILITY FOR THE JOURNEY AHEAD.

Vision provides an image of the future that produces strength of resolve and stability of character. These qualities can sustain a lifetime of service to others. Adolph Coors IV learned this truth through the death of his father.

> Daddy didn't come home. And the bullets that tore the life from his body also tore the life from his family. We had an ideal family and were living the American Dream. We had the home in the mountains, wealth, social status, and parents who loved us and took time to let us know their love. My life was almost everything a boy could want. Then on February 9, 1960, our world was ripped apart. That morning Adolph Herman Joseph Coors III left his mountain ranch at the usual 7:30 a.m. It was only twelve miles from the ranch to the Coors brewery in Golden, Colorado, and a short pleasant drive on a crisp winter morning. He would be early for work—as usual. But Adolph Coors III, president of the brewery his grand-father had begun in an abandoned tannery in 1873, never arrived at his office.[4]

Adolph Coors III never returned home. Joseph Corbett, an escaped convict from California, assaulted and killed him in a failed kidnap-for-ransom attempt. Seven months later, his remains were found by a hunter. His widow turned to alcohol, and his son, Adolph IV, was driven by bitterness to make his mark in life. Joseph Corbett was found in Canada, extradited to Colorado, and given a life sentence.

My first introduction to Adolph Coors IV was on October

27, 1989, when he spoke at a Gathering breakfast at the Athletic Club of Columbus. He told our audience, "I wished someone had loved me enough to invite me to a breakfast like this earlier in my life. I've made every mistake in the book. I have a message for all the successful and pleasant people in life: There is only one thing that goes in the box at the end of life . . . you and me! We work all our lives spending money we don't have, for things that we don't need, in order to gain the approval of people we don't even like. I was just like O. J. Simpson, who once said at the height of his career as a running back for the Buffalo Bills, 'I have all the success and fame in life and yet I'm lonely as hell.' I was just like Elvis Presley; I was rich and famous but deeply unhappy."

Seventeen years after that day in February 1960, as a thirty-one-year-old adult, Adolph Coors IV had a vision of becoming a millionaire. He went to college for one year but dropped out because he was majoring in "fraternity and sorority." He became a U.S. Marine and grew his physique from 190 pounds to 272 pounds with twenty-inch biceps and a fifty-four-inch chest.

> He could pound any man into submission, but he was unhappy.
>
> He became a millionaire, but he was unfulfilled.
>
> He married and had children, but he could not find peace.

During one difficult period of work, he went without sleep for three nights and had a head-on collision while driving home that left him unconscious for a week. The damage to his body required two years of strenuous recovery. Later, on the verge of divorce, his wife, B. J., invited a couple over for dinner to see if they could help salvage something of the Coors's marriage. Adolph was offered a new vision through a relationship with God, but chose to move out and take a room at the Denver Athletic Club. For the next six weeks, he lived inside his self-imposed sentence of loneliness and guilt, but finally called B. J. and asked to come home.

During his absence, B. J. responded to the quiet, faithful testimony of their friends, Lowell and Vera Sun, and began a personal relationship with God. It was not filled with tradition and custom, but with personal relevance and depth. Adolph followed her in faith in June 1975. He said, "I finally gave in, I finally responded to the knock of Jesus on my life. When I opened my life to his love, my deep void was instantly filled with a love that no person, no thing, no title, or no possession had been able to fill. For the first time in life I had a real purpose for living."

Strength of resolve and stability of character have sustained Adolph and B. J. Coors on their life journey ever since.

Adolph permanently separated himself from the family brewing business and has pursued a career as founder of the national marketing company, ADCO Enterprises. He has chosen to do this with only his wife and children. He gave up prestigious community and corporate boards to serve Prison Fellowship and Kanakuk Kamp for boys and girls. He walked away from the applause and accolades that so often come with fame and fortune to introduce people to God.

He reminded us over breakfast that morning of C. S. Lewis's statement, "If you live for the next world you get this one in the deal; but if you live only for this world, you end up losing them both." For years, his life was motivated by anger. After encountering God, he realized that "anger is an acid that can do far more harm to the vessel in which it is stored than to anything on which it is poured."

Two years later, his vision of "serving self through power and personal possessions" had been replaced by "telling God's love story to others." As a result, Adolph went to meet Joseph Corbett, his father's murderer, at the Colorado State Penitentiary. But Mr. Corbett would not see him. In place of a face-to-face meeting, Adolph wrote him a letter asking for his forgiveness "for the hatred I had been harboring for seventeen years. I told him I had forgiven him. As I walked from the prison, I felt God's love and I was a free man."

How do you forgive someone who killed your father? It must require incredible personal strength. How do you live each day in the aftermath of such tragedy? It must require a stability that only God can grant. Adolph Coors IV received God's forgiveness. His new life is sustained by strength and character forged over years of faithfully extending forgiveness to others.

Here is a short review of what we've learned about vision:

1. Vision enables us to focus on what is not yet as if it were already present. It gives us an image of the future that frees us from distractions and competing demands of life so that we can focus on achievable ends that are fulfilled in service to others.

2. Vision motivates us to take redemptive action in the world. It provides us with an image of the future that generates a determined and meaningful course of action that finds its fulfillment in service to others.

3. Vision strengthens and stabilizes us for the journey of life. It gives us an image of the future that produces strength of resolve and stability of character that will sustain us during our lifetime of service to others.

These three principles of vision are essential to staying on course in life. When I doubt or question my vision, I often turn to a passage in the Bible that challenges me to keep on keeping on. It's found in Joel 2:28-32, and it reminds me of three characteristics of true vision:

1. *It starts with God:* "I will pour out my Spirit" (v. 28).

2. *It's available to all:* "I will pour out my Spirit on all people. Your sons and daughters will prophesy, your old men will dream dreams, your young men will see visions. Even on my servants, both men and women, I will pour out my Spirit in those days" (vv. 28-29).

3. *It's revealed in service to others:* "Everyone who calls on the name of the LORD will be saved; for on Mount Zion and in Jerusalem there will be deliverance, as the LORD has said, among the survivors whom the LORD calls" (v. 32).

This is refreshing reassurance that you and I, as ordinary, every-day people, can make a difference, do make a difference, and will make a difference if we take God at his word and leave the known for the unknown under his direction. ✓

How big is your vision? Does your vision require God in order for it to be fulfilled? Is it big enough to inspire others to join you? If it's not big, then it's not a vision.

One final thought . . .

Billy Graham came to Columbus in 1993 for a five-day crusade that was attended by 175,000 people. Those five short days required five years of work. It began when five men met for prayer, and it concluded with 1,000 volunteers, 923 churches, and various businesses, members of Congress, and the governor participating. We could not have reached such heights had we crafted a doable vision. We reached beyond our grasp to impact an entire region of the United States, and people around the world were included by television. I still meet people today whose lives were changed during those five days in September.

Shortly after Dr. Graham left, he sent a video that we showed to community leaders later that fall. He left us with a vision that, apart from God's intervention, exceeded our grasp. He said, "You are the generation of leaders that God has raised up for this time. You will chart the course of history for Columbus, for Ohio, and possibly for the entire nation. You have a privilege to serve others and a corresponding burden to do so with love, humility, and justice."

Many of us are seeking to fulfill this vision. ✓

REFLECTIONS

Do you have a vision that fills you with passion for serving others?

What is your vision?

You might begin by saying, "I have a dream . . ."

WHY ON EARTH AM I HERE?

ANSWERING LIFE'S GREATEST QUESTION

*It's a riddle, wrapped in a mystery,
inside an enigma.*

—WINSTON CHURCHILL

IF YOU CAN answer the question "Why do I exist?" then you know your purpose in life. It's that simple. However, it's an intimidating question to ask of ourselves, and a demanding one to answer. It requires us to reach beyond the comfortable and sometimes superficial contingencies of everyday life to search out the deeper mysteries of our souls.

Why on earth am I here?

What is my purpose for being?

How can I know why I was created?

These questions take us to the end of ourselves and then expect more. They require us to investigate our view of the world. They cause us to question where we came from and why we were created. Such questions are not easily answered—and they call us to revisit our beliefs about God.

If we want a meaningful life, we must ask the difficult questions.

The late Winston Churchill, prime minister of Great Britain, in reflecting upon his relationship with the political and military leaders of Russia, was perplexed by their actions and described them as "a riddle, wrapped in a mystery, inside an enigma." That expression represents what I would call a trinity of confusion. We often feel this way when attempting to answer the question, why do I exist?

I believe that the enigma can be unwrapped and that we can understand the purpose for which we were created. God had a reason for creating us, and he placed a sense of purpose in our hearts. But it's up to us to discover what it is. Proverbs 20:5 affirms that "the purposes of a man's heart are deep waters, but a man of understanding draws them out." In other words, God has given us the ability to see his grand design, but he requires us to do the work of coming to understand it.

When we discover our purpose, it becomes the rudder that guides us through the waters of life. It sets our course and stabilizes us when the waves grow high or we encounter riptides. Dr. Myles Munroe, chairman of the International Third World Leaders Association, once told me, "The greatest tragedy in life is not death, but life without reason. It is dangerous to be alive and not know why you were given life. The deepest craving of the human spirit is to find a sense of significance and relevance. The search for relevance in life is the ultimate pursuit of mankind. There is something God has finished in you that you were born to start."[1]

We can learn from people who have gone before us in seeking God, who searched for the answers to life's big question and discovered a purpose worth more than life itself. This became their reason for existing. Part of the answer is common to all of us, and part of it is personally distinctive. ✓

❦

Maximilian Kolbe sought God's purpose for his life. He once said, "No one in the world can change truth. What we can do and should do is seek it and serve it where it is found." This statement sums up Kolbe's purpose—he was created to seek and serve truth wherever he found it. He believed in something beyond himself. He believed in something that would give life to others, though it cost him his own. He believed in God and in the truth that comes from him.

Maximilian Kolbe knew how to live because he was prepared to die.

Born in Poland on January 8, 1894, Kolbe contracted tuberculosis as a child, spent two years in a sanatorium, and remained in frail health his entire life. He pursued the ministry and was ordained a Catholic priest in Rome in 1918.[2]

Father Kolbe was an intellectual, journalist, and publisher who refused German citizenship and was considered a threat to the German occupation of Poland during the 1939 invasion. His monastery was ransacked, and he was transported to Amitz, where he was imprisoned for a time. On February 17, 1941, Father Maximilian was again arrested and charged with aiding Jews through the Polish underground. He was sent to prison in German-occupied Warsaw and suffered terribly at the hands of the brutal Nazi guards. On May 28, 1941, he and four companions were deported to Auschwitz.

Here he faced his greatest challenge and interior struggle, as he vividly reflects in his writings:

> The real conflict is inner conflict. Beyond armies of occupation and the catacombs of concentration camps, there are two irreconcilable enemies in the depth of every soul: good and evil, sin and love. And what are the victories on the battlefield if we ourselves are defeated in our innermost personal selves?[3]

And yet, his purpose and his God prevailed. Imprisoned in this awful death camp, Father Kolbe was given the striped convict uniform. Under the brutal leadership of Commandant Fritch, the Germans sought to render him powerless as prisoner number 16670, just another subhuman statistic waiting to die. Like others, he was forced into hard labor, carrying blocks of stone for the construction of a crematorium where many would breathe their last.

During roll call one July morning at cell block fourteen, it was discovered that a prisoner had escaped. As a result, all block fourteen prisoners were commanded to stand at attention until 3:00 that afternoon. Since the escapee eluded capture, ten were chosen at random to be put in isolation and starved to death, as punishment for the man who escaped and to deter future attempts.

Francis Gajowniczek was one of the ten prisoners chosen to die. When selected, he cried out, "My poor wife, my poor children, what will happen to my family?"

At that moment, another prisoner stepped forward. The ranting Fritch bellowed, "What does this Polish pig want?"

Father Kolbe responded, "I am a Catholic priest from Poland. I would like to take his place, because he has a wife and children." Astonished and yet somehow swayed, Fritch returned

Gajowniczek to his place in line, and Kolbe was sentenced to death in the starvation bunker. They had no food, clothing, water, or bedding, and there was only one outcome for all who entered: agony and certain death.

From the time that Kolbe descended into his death chamber, a change took place throughout the camp. The wailing and crying of the hopeless were replaced by prayers and hymns, and Fritch ceased his policy of taking ten victims to their death in place of escapees. The other nine all died before Kolbe, who remained alive for two weeks. On the morning of August 14, 1941, in need of space for additional starvation victims, the director of the infirmary injected the priest with a lethal dose of carbolic acid. Maximilian extended his arm to receive his death as his final act of submission to God.[4] Francis Gajowniczek, the man whose death sentence Maximilian served, survived the war and lived until 1995. Fifty-four years of life were granted to him and his family by the selfless, loving act of one man who fully understood his purpose. Kolbe was so confident of God's love that he embraced death unfettered by attachment to this world. He had answered the question, why do I exist? and was satisfied that the answer was more important than life. What confidence, humility, and faith!

When you and I reflect on the value we place on human life, especially our own, it seems impossible to measure. If God were to offer you something more valuable than life, would you want it? What if it led you to a place of peace and satisfaction, fulfillment, contentment, and the ability to love others? Would you take it?

If your answer is yes, then let the journey continue. ✓

Purpose can be defined as the object for which something exists or is done. It can also mean the original intent for which something was created. We were created by God, and we carry his purpose in us, so our purpose is fulfilled when we serve a cause higher than ourselves. I believe that you and I and all of humanity carry a common life purpose that takes precedence above all else.

It is, first, to know, love, enjoy, and serve God.

A football coach named Jim Tressel believes that "our lives, lived in pursuit of God's purpose, are the legacy we leave behind."[5]

Jim is the head football coach at Ohio State University. Every year, *the* game in the Big Ten Conference and in all of college football is OSU vs. Michigan. At OSU, coaches with more losses than wins over Michigan get fired, even if they have a winning season. It's just that important to the football fans of Ohio State. At a recent function, Coach Tressel said, "You all know that in 261 days we play Michigan. And you all know that the coach can be officially pronounced dead if he doesn't win that game!"

Coach knows the value of beating Michigan, and he knows something of greater value that he had to discover for himself.

Jim was an ordinary boy born to average parents of simple means in Mentor, Ohio. He was the son of a football coach, and his greatest desire was to be the next Rex Kern. Rex quarterbacked the Ohio State University Buckeye football team to a 27-16 victory over the University of Southern California Trojans to win the collegiate national title at the 1968 Rose Bowl.

On January 3, 2003, this same boy, now a man, coached the Buckeyes to a dramatic, heart-stopping double overtime 31-24 win over the heavily favored Miami University Hurricanes. There was a crowd of 77,501 in Sun Devil Stadium in Tempe, Arizona, and a television audience of millions worldwide. This event completed an undefeated season and their first national title since Rex Kern quarterbacked the team in 1968.

During Jim's twenty-one years as a head coach—fifteen at Division 1-AA Youngstown State University and six so far at

Ohio State—his teams have competed for the national title on eight separate occasions and have won it five times. He has been voted National Coach of the Year five times. According to the Buckeye faithful, any year that Michigan is defeated is a great year. Any year that OSU defeats Michigan and Penn State, wins the Big Ten Conference championship, goes undefeated, wins games without scoring an offensive touchdown, and beats a heavily favored opponent in double overtime to win the national title is indescribable. Coach Tressel has just about done it all. The next stop will be the College Football Hall of Fame!

On Thursday morning, March 6, 2003, he stepped to the podium to address a breakfast audience of four thousand at The Gathering. Since Coach Tressel is a proven winner at any level he has coached, I'm sure that many in the audience were wondering if he would talk about winning. Would he say that winning is everything? Could anything be more important?

What he said reflected his life's purpose.

Coach was very direct in his remarks. He revealed no secret plays and told no stories about wins over Michigan. He mentioned the national title only briefly. He began where his story of purpose began, because this was more important to him than all the wins, titles, and trophies.

He told us that as a teenager, he sought to emulate Rex Kern. He wanted to improve as a quarterback and please his high school coach. He attended a Fellowship of Christian Athletes camp at age fifteen because he knew that Rex was involved with FCA. He would do anything to follow in his hero's footsteps—even go to a religious sports camp. He would also do whatever it took to be a winner.

One of the speakers at that sports camp was Bobby Richardson, a ten-time World Series participant with the New York Yankees. During his talk, Bobby asked the campers a compelling question:

"If the game of life were to end tonight, would you be a winner?" Young Jim thought long and hard, and discovered that he didn't have an answer. Bobby said that the answer to being a winner in life was found in a relationship with God. Jim chose "winning at life" that night over winning at football. He has chosen to let God direct his life ever since.

Coach was quick to remind us on that cold, snowy morning that it had not been easy. He told us that he had not been perfect, admitting, "I have a lot of 'fan mail' to prove it!" But he recited a poem for us to underscore the value of his relationship with God:

> *The Hall of Fame is only good as long as time shall be,*
> *but keep in mind God's Hall of Fame is for eternity.*
> *To have your name inscribed up there is greater more by far*
> *than all the praise and all the fame of any manmade star.*

Coach Tressel continued his story:

> The beauty of God's Hall of Fame is that we can all make it. It isn't reserved only for the exceptional athlete or the extremely gifted. Life is a mixture of good and bad, but no matter what happens, God never leaves us. All of life that holds meaning and purpose is centered in knowing God, loving God, and serving God upon whatever platform he places you. The real bottom line is not winning the National Championship and it's not beating Michigan. It's found in a relationship with God.

He also told us that before each home game the team makes one final act of commitment before taking the field. They recite an Edward Hale poem that is posted on the locker room wall:

I am only one—but I am one.
I can't do everything, but I can do something.
That I can do I ought to do.
And what I ought to do
by the grace of God
I shall do.

Let's reflect on this for a minute. This poem tells me that our purpose is only revealed to the world when we do something. Our "knowing, loving, and serving God" takes form and gives life to us and to others only through redemptive action that sets others free to be restored to God.

Coach Tressel is a mentor, teacher, character builder, husband, father, and much more than a football coach. His purpose takes him beyond the glory of the gridiron. He knows that beating Michigan is critically important to an OSU head football coach, but he is ultimately guided by a desire to leave the legacy of a life lived for God.

Jim Tressel's life purpose is found in knowing God, loving God, and serving God. He left us that morning with something eternal that would make us better people, not better fans. He served us, his purpose, and God very well.

I use the word *enjoy* as part of our common purpose, but Coach didn't mention this in his message. He didn't need to—it was written all over his face. When we do what we were created to do, we will have joy and satisfaction.

Our purpose, far more than a duty, can seem to be life itself.

For too long, I thought I had to do things for God, and I found this an obligation and an effort. Now, I seek to express the purpose that God has placed within me, and when I do, he gives me joy. ✓

We share a common purpose with all humanity, but the second aspect of our life purpose is individual. Each of us is uniquely designed and created with gifts, abilities, interests, strengths, and weaknesses. I am different than you, and you are different than me. One of our biggest challenges is to discover who we were created to be, and then to become that person. Our purpose is not to do what someone else does or be who someone else is, but to understand and fulfill the unique purpose placed in each of us.

You are here for a reason. You are not a mistake, regardless of the circumstances surrounding your conception, birth, and childhood.

You are here because you have something that the world needs.

Discovering our individual purpose takes us on a journey that will include some bruises and bumps. God sometimes takes us through difficult circumstances to prepare, refine, and develop us. You are not fully developed at the beginning of your relationship with God. As you grow, the purpose within you grows as it is challenged and tested by the people, events, and circumstances of life. I have certainly had my share of hard knocks.

Many years ago, Rita and I vacationed along the coast of Maine. As I looked out to sea, felt the sun and wind, watched seagulls, and smelled the salty air, I heard a rumbling sound that would increase, stop suddenly, and then start up again, receding in intensity.

When I took a closer look, I saw that the waves were gathering thousands of rocks and throwing them repeatedly against the cliffs. I reached into the water and pulled out a smooth, rounded rock that perfectly fit my hand. What was once ragged and sharp had been reshaped and smoothed over time. Its final form came from being repeatedly scraped, ground, and bumped against thousands of other rocks and against the high shoreline cliffs that ended its journey from sea to land.

This rock sits on my desk. The sharp-edged rock that it once was would never have fit in my hand or have rested easily on my desk. It was molded and shaped over time.

God polishes off our rough edges, transforms us, and readies us for action, so that we can accomplish his purposes. "He chose us in him before the creation of the world to be holy and blameless in his sight. In him we were also chosen, having been predestined according to the plan of him who works out everything in conformity with the purpose of his will" (Ephesians 1:4, 11). You are God's planned and chosen child, and he wants to realize part of his dream through you.

God, who is love, created us to live in relationship with him, so we can rest assured that he has our best interests at heart. When we seek his best for ourselves, we discover our purpose. We may not begin with a clear understanding of God's intentions, but we can get to know the God who has plans for our lives.

God walks through life with you because you are valuable to him. God has placed a plan within you that you were born to bring to light. This is your purpose for being. If it is not realized, you will exist, but you will never be fully alive. ✓

REFLECTIONS

In the movie Chariots of Fire, *the actor who portrays Olympic runner Eric Liddell tells his sister that when he runs he feels God's pleasure. What do you do in your life where you feel God's pleasure?*

What in life are you most willing to live for?

What is your purpose for being?

MISSION POSSIBLE!

WHAT WOULD JESUS (HAVE YOU) DO?

*What I really lack is to be clear in my mind what I am to do,
not what I am to know. The thing is to understand myself,
to see what God really wishes me to do, to find the idea for
which I can live and die.*

—SØREN KIERKEGAARD

SEVERAL YEARS AGO, I read a book called *Ghost Soldiers,* by
Hampton Sides, which tells the story of a daring mission undertaken during World War II to rescue some of the last survivors
of the Bataan Death March in the Philippines. I was intrigued
by the account and later wrote the following summary to try to
capture the experience from inside the hearts and minds of the
prisoners of war and of those who risked their lives to bring them
to safety.

We were the most pitiful of all survivors—the emaciated, sick, disabled, and mentally unstable remnant-survivors of the Bataan Death March. Captured and conscripted to build a jungle airstrip for the enemy, my fellow countrymen, soldiers, and allied friends and I were then forced into trenches, drenched with aviation fuel, and set on fire. Those who managed to escape the pit and breach the surrounding barbed wire fence of our internment camp were massacred as they fled, or beheaded when their hiding places were discovered. And yet somehow, some way, some of my mates and I miraculously made it back to the American side to tell our story.

We had fought on the islands and in the jungles of the Philippines at the beginning of World War II, and we had lost. We were participants in the greatest defeat in U.S. military history. Our captors were soldiers of the Imperial Army of Japan. We were now imprisoned at Cabanatuan Camp. What had once been as many as 8,000 Americans was now down to 513. The Imperial Army had sent all able-bodied prisoners to Japan to work the mines or load warships.

During our three week, seventy-five mile "death march" along the Bataan peninsula, nearly six thousand of my comrades had died or were executed . . . one fallen soldier for every twenty paces of the journey. And once in camp, the deaths continued. It was common for two men to become very close. It was common that when one buddy became sick and died, the other would pass within hours or days. We were kept in units of ten. If one man escaped or attempted escape, his nine comrades were executed. That was our yesterday, that was our today, that was our tomorrow, that was our fate—or so we thought.

We didn't know that we were about to become the focus of the greatest rescue mission of World War II . . .

We were 121 hand-selected Rangers, accompanied by some eighty guerrilla fighters, Filipino soldiers, and civilians armed with everything from machine guns, bazookas, and explosives to small arms, knives, and sticks. The fate of 513 POWs, some thirty miles behind enemy lines, rested in our hands.

General Douglas MacArthur was about to return and launch an invasion of epic scale, and Cabanatuan was in its path. We feared that once the Japanese became aware of MacArthur's intentions, all prisoners would be killed. We knew that some seven thousand Japanese troops had amassed at Cabanatuan City, just four miles from the prison, and one thousand additional soldiers were at the Cabu River, just a mile away, so our mission and the lives of the prisoners were greatly imperiled. Somehow we had to travel undetected for thirty miles over difficult terrain, overpower an unknown number of enemy soldiers at the camp, avoid battle engagement with the thousands of other Japanese soldiers nearby, and safely evacuate the grievously undernourished and nearly dead men who remained.

Our guerrilla fighters guided us undetected to our target, fording streams, crossing roads, and avoiding patrols. We undertook reconnaissance of our objective, unaware as we inched across the ground around the prison wire that we were crawling over the mass graves of our brothers.

When darkness fell, we struck, cutting the telephone wires to Cabanatuan City and praying that the Japanese battalions there would not be roused—miraculously they were not. We blew up the bridge between the camp and the detachment of soldiers at the Cabu River and cut down their advancement with our bazookas and machine guns in an enormous firefight. We opened fire on the guard posts and the sleeping quarters with such a massive and violent force that there was little response. We guided the dazed and confused prisoners to the front gate—many who thought it was just another deceptive trick of the enemy. We enlisted villagers, fifty slow-moving water buffalo, carts, tree limbs, sticks, and even doors upon which to carry our frail cargo. We traveled all night, amazed at the ability of so many to take so many steps when their bodies were so feeble and weak, and walking on swollen and bleeding feet. Our thirty-mile return trip was cut to fifteen when the front line of the American offensive was able to advance fifteen miles closer to our position over the next three days.

And finally . . . finally, we were met in our "life march" by our own troops, and at last we were safe. We lost four men that night, two Rangers killed in action and two prisoners who were too weak and debilitated to survive the journey. At last we hugged, we cried, we laughed, we slept, and we ate—boy, did we eat.

Mission accomplished![1]

The point I want to make with this story is this: Had the Rangers pursued their rescue mission without a focused objective, reconnaissance, preparation, or faith in themselves and one another, every prisoner would surely have lost his life. ✓

I don't believe that you and I can succeed in our life purpose without a focused objective. We must choose a course of action for our lives and have faith in ourselves, others, and God. That's why we need a mission.

Mission can be defined as a sending out with authority to perform a special duty, or the special duty or function for which someone is sent. Have you discovered your assignment or special duty in life? Are you pursuing it with authority? Are you doing what Jesus would have you do?

In the preceding chapters, we talked about purpose, a persistent, internal thread of reason, passion, and motivation that pervades your entire being, past, present, and future. We also discussed vision, a picture of the future that God has called you to. We now take a look at mission, which is the specific task or duty that God directs you to do today, tomorrow, and beyond.

Mission addresses the question of how I live out my purpose in the world today. It is outward-focused action that is consistent with your life purpose. Mission is what others see when you pursue your vision and purpose.

In the January/February 2004 issue of *New Man* magazine, John Maxwell—author, speaker, and leadership development expert—reflects on the value of knowing and embarking upon your life's mission. He writes, "You can't borrow another person's mission. And no one but God can give it to you. But there are some common themes that run through the life of every person of purpose: (1) Your mission is bigger than a single goal. (2) Your mission will require a positive attitude. (3) Your mission will develop over time."[2]

These insights may more easily be understood when they are illustrated by the lives of some people you may know or have heard about.

I'm not Greek, and I've never run a marathon, but I can learn a lot from someone who ran a marathon while pursuing a seemingly impossible mission.

∽

On April 20, 1946, two-time Greek Olympian Stylianos Kyriakides won the fiftieth Boston Marathon, a race he had lost eight years before. This time, he had the fastest time in the world posted for 1946, and he defeated the defending champion. For Kyriakides, this event was about much more than winning a race. He is a perfect example of someone with a personal mission that became larger than an individual goal.

Like millions of other civilians in early 1940s Europe, Kyriakides was caught in the grip of Nazi Germany occupation. On one occasion, he and a group of companions were imprisoned and charged with the death of a German soldier. When they were questioned, he alone was released, because he had run the marathon for Greece in the Berlin Olympics.

The next day, he was horrified to discover that each of his buddies had been hanged in the public square. Devastated by his loss and a sense of guilt at being the sole survivor, he desperately wanted to contribute something to the greater good of his country.

What could he do? Where would he start?

Greece was facing civil war, and thousands were dying of disease, neglect, and starvation. With the burden of his country on his shoulders, Kyriakides decided to run.

He entered the 1946 Boston Marathon to awaken the world to the needs of his people and to raise funds for his beloved homeland. For him, this was a mission of compassion. He came to the United States with the help of benefactors, having not run in six years.

He was thin and in poor health, and doctors at first told him that he would not be allowed to run for fear that he might die on the streets of Boston. He ran, came on at the end to win in world-class time, and raised three million dollars for the people of Greece.

Upon his return to Greece in May 1946, he was met by nearly a million people who celebrated his heart, his mission, and the donations of food, clothing, and medicine that were needed for their health and well-being. His mission was not just to win the Boston Marathon, the gold, or the glory. It was about raising awareness of his people's plight.[3]

Is your life mission bigger than a single goal?

Does it have an outward focus that benefits those in your world?

Has God given it to you? ✓

∞

I wish I could tell you that I knew Greg Schworm far better than I did. One thing he left with me was the reality that "every second counts." He only said it to me once, but that's all it took to indelibly write it on my heart. He deeply understood that any mission worth having requires a positive attitude. In the short time that we traveled together, he had a revitalizing effect on me.

On Monday, May 31, 2004, Greg lost his battle with cancer. He left us on a high note—just ask his wife, Martha, or any other family member. Greg, Martha, and I had lunch several months before his death, and I left the table refreshed.

Greg volunteered for a number of events for The Gathering that required him to rise early, travel downtown, perform the monotonous task of distributing literature on some four hundred tables at 5:30 A.M., and then greet and guide people to their seats in time for the 7:30 A.M. breakfast. He smiled, encouraged, and offered hope to others without focusing on his terminal condition.

Did I tell you that we had dessert with our lunch? You couldn't avoid Greg's infectious enthusiasm. When you were with Greg, you ordered dessert! On occasion, he would say, "Eat dessert first!" And he would. He understood the value of the moment, the value of *living*.

We shared a common interest in music, including that of Elvis Presley, so Greg told me to go to Graceland, Elvis's home. He and Martha had already made the trip. It was just that simple to him. Drink in life and God's love, and then empty all of it into the lives of others before the end of the day. He wasn't waiting for life to arrive; he had punched his ticket, gotten on board, and set the pace!

On June 5, Russ Corley, a mutual friend of ours, presided at Greg's memorial service. He reminded us that Greg had not always had such an attitude, and then he revisited Greg's transformation for us:

> Cancer came and altered everything. For months, the cancer was a dark tomb, an emotional chaos as well as a destructive physical enemy. But at some point, after surgery and a long hard struggle at home, and after a devastating round of chemotherapy, there was a miracle. The Gospel of John tells the story of Lazarus, a man who had been dead for four days. But then Jesus came, had the stone rolled away, and called Lazarus forth!
>
> Greg was Lazarus! He stepped out of a premature tomb named cancer and moved among us with New Life—the eternal "enfleshed" in the present. Everything else was similar, but Greg was altered at the core of his being. He had no more fear or anxiety, and his life was permeated with a faithful joy, a hopeful confidence, and an authentic love. He was the bearer of genuine Good News that each

day was a precious gift from God—and one to be lived
fully! He saw each person as a valued, unique individual
to be cherished. He became the incarnation of God's love,
the person of Christ dwelling among us.[4]

If God is within you, shouldn't someone see that? When someone
looks you in the eye, catches the tone of your voice, or enters your
presence, what do they encounter? Is there a sparkle, a hint of
laughter, a permeating joy? It makes a difference that no human
instrument can measure!

So what's for dessert?

Have you been to Graceland?

Does every second count? ✓

ACTIONS

Write down your answers to the following questions:

How do you want your purpose to be reflected in your life?

How do you want your purpose to be reflected in your family?

How do you want your purpose to be reflected in your career?

"SUCCESS" IS OPTIONAL

LETTING YOUR MISSION DEVELOP

*I will study and get ready, and
the opportunity will come.*

—ABRAHAM LINCOLN

EARLIER, I MENTIONED John Maxwell's belief that your mission
will develop over time. Let me now introduce you to a friend and
former football player and the story of his developing mission. I
think it will help you to better understand this idea.

He walked into the ballroom of the Hyatt Regency Columbus
on Thursday morning, May 2, 2002, to tell his story. It was
direct, authentic, and passionate, because that is how he was.
Some of us saw his picture on the cereal box as we ate a bowl of
Wheaties in our younger days—he was seventeen at the time. He
was a throwback to an earlier work ethic of discipline, team play,
and respect for the game.

He was a football player named Chris Spielman: high school stud, two-time All-American at Ohio State University, and the winner of the Lombardi Trophy his senior year. He was "too small" for professional football yet he achieved success as a four-time All-Pro who played eleven years in the NFL, leading the Detroit Lions in tackles for nine consecutive seasons.

Chris was passionately living the dream with a beautiful wife, children, and career. On a Sunday afternoon in the fall of 1997, as Chris sat in the visiting team's locker room of the RCA Dome preparing to play the Indianapolis Colts, God interrupted his pre-game routine.

What are you on earth for, Chris?

Chris responded, "Not now . . . don't you understand? I have to prepare to tackle Marshall Faulk [running back for the Colts]. I can't solve life's mystery right now!"

He didn't have time. He was about to enter a violent arena of physical survival where six-foot-six-inch men weighing 315 pounds would be coming at him with bad intentions, and he would need his own set of bad intentions if he were to survive. The voice returned, but he once again put it off. In the fourth period, he tackled Lamont Warren. "I couldn't feel anything from my neck down for two seconds, but I shook it off, got up, and finished the game."

A few months later, Chris was informed by their doctor that his wife, Stefanie, had breast cancer.

"I punched the window; I was angry and cried: 'My neck, your cancer, why is this happening to us?'

"Stefanie looked right at me, and said, 'How dare you, how dare you, with all the blessings that have been given to us?' Right then I saw a picture of service that I could not match."

Chris took the next year off from professional football to care for Stefanie and the kids.

"When my children came down the stairs with hair in their mouths from the chemotherapy and they wanted to know what was wrong with Mommy, who else would there have been to tell them? What a fake and a fraud and a phony I would have been if I went off to play a game instead of playing the game of life with my family."

One night Chris couldn't sleep. As he sought relief by watching the golf channel, Jesus showed up on his couch.

"In my mind, it was Jesus sitting over on the couch. I was watching some guy hit a golf ball out of the back of a truck with a new club and knocking it two feet from the pin. I said to Jesus, 'I don't think that even you can make that shot,' to which he responded, 'Don't bet on it!'"

Chris asked Jesus to get Stefanie through the chemo and the cancer by his taking half of the burden and Jesus taking the other half.

And then Jesus was gone.

The cancer was gone.

The football career resumed.

The neck was reinjured.

The football career was over.

Stefanie was pregnant.

Stefanie's cancer returned in 2001. Chris says, "I took the kids to school and rolled up into a fetal position in my car. I couldn't go on. I couldn't do it any more. I couldn't go through it again.

I gave it all to God, not just half, but all of it to him this time. I prayed that Stefanie would be healed by God to be used as his messenger this time, not for me and my benefit, but for God and his purposes as a beacon of hope of what is possible through faith."

As of this writing, Stefanie's cancer has returned, but she is still fighting, living, and loving. Chris is a college football analyst for ESPN and hosts a daily sports talk show. Stefanie is mom to their four children and offers hope to victims of breast cancer and their families.

The following, written by Chris, reflects the growth and transformation of his mission over time.

> *What Am I?*
> *Detroit Lions, 1996*
> *I am a professional football player.*
> *I say that with all the pride, honor, and humility that title deserves.*
> *I will always give 100 percent, both mentally and physically, to my team.*
> *Challenges will be met without hesitation or fear for my team.*
> *Team success will always be a prerequisite to personal success for my team.*
> *My team's glory will be my glory.*
> *This I pledge—Chris Spielman.*
>
> *What Am I?*
> *Buffalo Bills, 1997*
> *I am a husband and a father.*
> *I say that with all the pride, honor, and humility that title deserves.*

*I will always give 100 percent, both mentally and physically,
    to my family.*
*Challenges will be met without hesitation or fear for my
    family.*
My family's glory will always be a prerequisite to personal glory.
My family's glory will be my glory.
This I pledge—Chris Spielman.

What Am I?
Sports Radio Talk Show Host, 2002
I am a Christian man.
*I say that with all the pride, honor, and humility that title
    deserves.*
*I will always give 100 percent, both mentally and physically,
    to God.*
Challenges will be met without hesitation or fear for God.
God's glory will always be a prerequisite to personal glory.
God's glory will be my glory.
This I pledge—Chris Spielman.

Chris finished by saying, "People hold us up on a pedestal. It's not easy, and it's embarrassing, but hopefully we can set the same kind of example that Jesus did some two thousand years ago." Chris's awareness of his mission in life—to serve God, family, and community—grew over time as he was gradually brought closer to God, and as God used the circumstances of his life and the witness of others.[1] ✓

You don't have to figure it all out today. Your understanding of your mission doesn't require you to have a certain number of words that fit your thoughts neatly, sound wonderful as they roll off your tongue, or look great on a sheet of paper. But you must begin to seek and pursue your mission. When you do, you will find God, and when you find him, you will discover your mission.

Give it time, but don't waste time. ✓

This next story about mission is about a place that you and I visit from time to time—a place called failure. Your mission just might take you there.

For many people, I suppose, Hudson Taylor is no longer a household name. But his efforts as a missionary to China during the 1800s planted seeds that are still bearing fruit to this day. Born in 1832, in Barnsley, England, Taylor was raised in a Christian home. His father was a pharmacist and a lay Methodist preacher, and his mother was deeply devout. Hudson himself went through a period of adolescent rebellion, but when he was fifteen, he experienced a dramatic conversion through the reading of a gospel tract. Not long after this, he began to prepare for his life's work as a missionary to China. He studied Chinese, Greek, Hebrew, and Latin, and began training to be a physician, but left in 1853 before completing his studies. He went to Nanking, China, as a missionary to the Taiping people at the ripe old age of twenty-one years, ten months. He adopted the dress and lifestyle of the people he wanted to reach.

Hudson Taylor encountered civil war and realized that the rebels only embraced Jesus in a nominal way, and often for political reasons. He was miserable and homesick, and he suffered severe headaches and constant cold. In spite of these setbacks, he traveled throughout the interior of China, preaching and encouraging other missionaries. He traveled back and forth between England and China eleven separate times during his life.

Taylor was attacked, lost all of his worldly possessions, and was cut off from his overseas missionary salary. He continued to preach and offer medical services wherever he could. He suffered separation from his family, depression, illness, and grave disappointment. Time after time, his efforts failed to turn the spiritual tide of this huge nation.

Civil war followed civil war. Sickness followed sickness. Failure followed failure. Taylor's daughter died from water on the brain, and the entire family was almost killed in the Yang Chow Riot of 1868. Maria, Taylor's first wife, died in childbirth, and his second wife died of cancer.

Desperately seeking God's peace through the difficulties, loss, and failures of his mission work, he finally came to this realization: "I have striven in vain to abide in him; I'll strive no more. For has not he promised to abide with me . . . never to leave me, never to fail me?" Hudson Taylor's failures led him to a new peace and a new depth in his relationship with God.

Ill health required his return to England. This setback to his work resulted in his completing his medical studies, revising the Chinese New Testament, and organizing the China Inland Mission to carry the gospel where it had never been before. By 1895, the mission had 641 missionaries and 462 Chinese helpers at 260 stations. Under Hudson Taylor's leadership, the CIM supplied over half of the Protestant missionary force in China.

During the Boxer Rebellion of 1900, fifty-six of these missionaries were martyred, and hundreds of Chinese Christians were killed. The missionary work did not slacken, however, and the number of missionaries quadrupled in the following decades. The humble, determined efforts of Hudson Taylor and those he recruited, supported, and guided gave birth to a living faith

in God for millions of Chinese believers in the decades that followed. The message of Jesus overcame oppression, government
sanction, and martyrdom.[2]

There were an estimated three million followers of Jesus in
China in 1949, when all public worship was banned except in
state-run churches. When Rita and I arrived in Hong Kong and
stepped onto the soil of mainland China for an international
conference in 1984, there were reportedly sixty million Chinese
believers, and today there are an estimated eighty to one hundred
million Christians in China.

Wouldn't you say that Hudson Taylor accomplished his mission? Wouldn't you say that he overcame failure? You and I need to
embrace a new paradigm—that with God all things are possible. ✓

Your mission requires God's participation.

Sometimes I can't find God when I look for him, and sometimes
he seems to be right at my elbow. Sometimes I sense him pulling
me forward, and sometimes I don't see him until I look back over
the circumstances of my life. I've come to realize that I can't accomplish my purpose, my vision, or my mission without him.

Sometimes I am in such need that he shows up powerfully and supernaturally. The following account is of one such
experience.

I took a phone call at 11:30 one night from some friends who
operate a halfway house for girls in the Denver area. One of their
girls was experiencing what they thought was a demonic attack,
and they were calling me to assist in a spiritual intervention. My
friends were aware of my background working with incarcerated
teens at the Denver Juvenile Hall, which had given me some
experience with young men and women who had suffered some

form of physical, sexual, emotional, or spiritual abuse, as well as some who had dabbled in occultic and demonic practices. In truth, I had a modest, but far more than average, amount of experience working with the demonic, but it was more than my friends had, and more than anyone else they knew. So they had called me.

As soon as they described the situation, a creeping coldness enveloped my body. I didn't want to face the conflict alone, so I called my buddy Gil Larribas, who had grown up in an inner-city environment and had experience in physically threatening situations, such as working on the streets with drug addicts and in prisons. He was savvy, wise, and more experienced in this area than anyone I knew, so I asked him to join me. Then I dressed and picked up my Bible to see how God might want to prepare me for the unknown.

Gil arrived shortly after midnight. We took my car and drove along Hampden Avenue in Littleton, Colorado to our appointment not far from the campus of Denver Seminary. We entered the group home and spoke briefly to the houseparents, who were caring for a number of teenage girl runaways, drug addicts, and victims of abuse. At least one of the girls was profoundly oppressed, if not possessed, by demons. The demons were clearly present—or at least one, for sure. The young girl wanted out of the demonic bonds, and she was willing to fight, pray, and give herself to Jesus.

It wasn't easy. The demon growled, shouted unintelligible utterances, and thrashed the girl's body about, leaving all of us subject to injury and harm. He would not go quickly, quietly, or without a fight.

It's a fearful thing to encounter Satan's forces, and it should never be taken lightly. If ever I felt unprepared for a challenge in life, this was the time. How do you fight the unseen? How do you engage the forces of darkness? How do you empty yourself so that you can be a pure vessel that God can use to bind and send away a demon? I must have missed that class in seminary! We gathered around the girl, laid hands on her, and prayed, and prayed, and prayed.

We believed God and took him at his word. We believed what he said in Matthew 17:20, "I tell you the truth, if you have faith as small as a mustard seed, you can say to this mountain, 'Move from here to there,' and it will." We called upon the presence of God; we beckoned the Holy Spirit to come. We claimed the blood of Jesus Christ and spoke in his name. God showed up. The demon held on and fought us . . . but God was there, his power prevailed, and the demonic forces were defeated.

At one point, God's presence was so overwhelming that I laughed as we were praying. It was an unbelievable moment that I could never explain. God was so real and powerful that my deep, deep fear was replaced by security in God, and I could laugh freely. I was freer at that moment than at any other time in my life, only because God showed up! It was the only way that we could meet the challenge—in our own strength, we would have failed.

I cannot tell you what ultimately became of that young girl, but I know that God was there that night. He moved in that room and in that girl, and for the coming days that demon was subdued and defeated. I also know that whatever challenge, obstacle, or goal lies in the path of your mission, it will only be met, overcome, or achieved by God's grace.

You may struggle with your own demons—either literal or figurative. They may lie in your path or be part of your history of bad choices. You may have to struggle with them for a while, but you do not have to struggle alone. They may deter you temporarily from achieving your mission, but they cannot prevent you from fulfilling it if you invite God to do for you what you cannot do for yourself. Sometimes it is in the struggle that our mission is revealed or confirmed. That was the experience of my mentor and friend, Tony Campolo.

Author, speaker, sociologist, and pastor Dr. Tony Campolo is a professor at Eastern University in St. Davids, Pennsylvania. When he was forty years old, he entered politics because he wanted to make a difference in the world, and his fifteen years of teaching sociology at the university level had left him questioning whether he wanted to be a sociologist for the rest of his life.

In 1976, he entered the race for a seat in the U.S. Congress from the Fifth District of Pennsylvania. He won the primary but was defeated in the general election. Reflecting on that period of his life, Dr. Campolo writes,

> As I look back on it all, I can honestly say that I'm glad I didn't win. If I had won, I might have been trapped into a track-for-life that would have kept me from what has given me a much fuller sense of joyful purpose. My friends forced me to set down on paper what I had been doing in life that had been *fun*. I know that *fun* sounds terribly unholy, but my friends and I are convinced that God has so designed us that what he has willed for us to do with our lives creates a sense of joy. Upon reflection, I realized that I got my greatest kicks out of talking to college students. My friends next helped me to zero in on the primary, most significant thing that I had accomplished through speaking to college students. I realized that this happened when I was able to get students to consider how their lives could be invested most effectively to impact others for Christ. I wanted them to become

missionaries! By the end of the afternoon, I had written out my mission for life, and I believe that it came from God. It reads: Before I hang up my sneakers at the end, I want to have motivated and helped at least 200 college and university students to commit themselves to going out as full-time missionaries for the cause of Christ.[3]

What does your mission statement look like? Have you written it down? Tony didn't take a close look at his until he was forced to do so, until he lost something that he thought would be his next success. When he did, he discovered that he was already pursuing his mission. It may be helpful for you to reflect on the mission statements of others to help you develop your own.

My mission is to be God's instrument in revealing his love to a lost world.

Why? Because I believe that God forgives my sins, heals my diseases, redeems my life, crowns me with love and compassion, and satisfies my desires. If this is what God has done for me, then why would I not want to share him with the world? That's what drives and motivates me. My mission has never changed, although I've worked with incarcerated kids, business and government leaders, and with the impoverished communities of Cielo and Nazaret in the Dominican Republic. The people may change, but my mission remains constant.

When I worked with Youth Guidance in the 1970s and 1980s, our mission was to provide hopeful alternatives to troubled young people and their families through caring relationships and developmental opportunities for the whole person (mental, social, physical, and spiritual). If I couldn't love a hurting kid, offer practical assistance to help them in their short- and long-term needs, enjoy them for who they were, and somehow be part of leading them to God, then I wasn't "on-mission."

In an earlier chapter, I introduced you to David Steward, chairman of World Wide Technology, Inc. WWT's mission statement is "to provide a revolutionary way to streamline and simplify the global IT chain, all from a single source—WWT."

Another example of *mission* comes from Material Assistance Providers, a local nonprofit organization serving the poor in central Ohio. Their mission is to serve the community by providing a free furniture bank for families and individuals in need.

Bob Buford, a man who made millions in the cable television business and now connects problems with problem solvers through an organization called Half Time, writes about mission in his book *Half Time,* "I like to think of myself as a strategic broker—someone who has the skills needed to link problem identifiers with problem solvers. This is how I am wired; this is what I did with my cable TV business, so my life mission necessarily relates to this role. My life mission is to transform the latent energy in American Christianity into active energy.[4]

In the Catholic Diocese of Columbus, the Catholic Men's mission statement is "to support, strengthen, and maximize the spiritual growth of Catholic men through prayer, Scripture reading, communication, and networking by sponsoring gatherings for all men."

Somewhere in these examples or in the preceding pages are the seeds of truth, the soil of provision, and the water of life necessary for you to cultivate, grow, and harvest your own life mission. Like so many of God's gifts, it comes to those who ask and seek.

What will you ask and what will you seek?

Is there already a sense in your soul that you understand what he is asking you to do? Why not write down your thoughts, entrust them to God, and see how he affirms them in your life—even today. ✓

REFLECTIONS

What is your life's mission?

What roles do compassion and justice play in your mission?

What role does love play in your mission?

ACTIONS

Write down three meaningful things in life that you have done that have been fun.

Write out how each of these things may tie into your mission.

Identify and write down three things you are going to do to fulfill your mission before the end of the year.

LOOKING UNDER THE HOOD

DISCOVERING YOUR GOD-GIVEN GIFTS

*It is God who works in you to will and to act
according to his good purpose.*

—PHILIPPIANS 2:13

I WROTE THE following words during a transitional time in my
life. I was facing a new city, state, and job, and the beginning
of a master's degree, and I was concerned that my abilities were
insufficient for the tasks ahead. When I took the focus off my
limitations and placed it on God and when I accepted myself, I
found freedom.

Talents
I am but a simple man
Wondering about my life's plan

What is it you'll have me do
I guess I'll have to wait on you.
My talents aren't in large reserve
I haven't the power of many words
I need some more to complete this phrase
And I have to finish the rest of the page.
Creativity isn't in me
I'm usually satisfied with letting things be
Knowledge doesn't quickly take my hand
As I said, I'm a simple man.
I doubt if I will ever be a leader
Or even come close to being Peter
I'm not witty or wise or overly smart
My talent will have to come from my heart.
I can give of my time, my effort, my love
I can give of myself, that there's plenty of
I can share with another in their time of grief
Maybe take them to you to give them relief.
It's best to be satisfied with me
Instead of fretting about who I should be
In living my life I'll look for your help
And accept myself.

NOVEMBER 21, 1977

I believe that the number one expert on you ought to be *you*.

In any understanding of your natural abilities and spiritual gifts, your first job is to accept yourself as the person God created you to be. Let me say it again: I believe that you should be the number one expert on yourself. If this is true, you must understand your gifts and abilities. We've all heard the phrase "It's not what you know, but who you know that counts." I'd like to revise that to say, "It's what you know *about who you are* that counts."

After all, if you become the "best you" possible, won't everyone else in your life benefit? Don't you owe it to those you know, and to those you will encounter later, to be the most self-aware, authentic person you can be? I believe that when your gifts and abilities are recognized and released with an active concern for others, you become the hands and feet that God uses to change humanity.

That's not just action. That's redemptive action.

When I reflect on the words of the opening poem, I see preoccupation with myself and a resultant negative comparison of myself with others. Whenever I do that, I lose, and when you do it, you lose, too. When we focus too much time on our weaknesses or on our differences from others, we always fall short. We end up serving doubt, depression, and failure.

Let me show you how disastrous this can be.

Willie Lynch was a skilled slave master. He was brought from the West Indian plantations to America in 1712 to deploy a system for controlling the behavior of slaves in Virginia. The following is part of what he said to a gathering of slave owners in what has come to be called The Speech:

> I am here to help you solve some of your problems with slaves. I caught a whiff of a dead slave hanging from a tree a couple of miles back. You are not only losing valuable stock by hangings, you are having uprisings, and your crops are sometimes left in the field too long. I am not here to enumerate your problems; I am here to introduce

you to a method of solving them. In my bag here I have
a fool-proof method for controlling your black slaves. I
guarantee every one of you that if installed correctly, it
will control the slaves for 300 years. My method is simple,
and members of your family can use it.

I have outlined a number of differences among the
slaves, and I take these differences and make them bigger.
I use fear, distrust, and envy for control. On top of my list
is "Age," but it is there only because it starts with an "A."
The second is "Color" or shade; there is intelligence, size,
sex, status, texture of hair, and tall or short. I shall give
you an outline of action, but before that, I shall assure
you that distrust is stronger than trust, and envy is stronger than adulation, respect, or admiration.

Don't forget you must pitch the old black vs. the young
black male. You must use the dark skin slaves vs. the light
skin slaves. You must also have your white servants and
overseers distrust all blacks, but it is necessary that your
slaves trust and depend on us. They must love, respect,
and trust only us.

Gentlemen, these kits are your keys to control, use
them. Have your wives and children use them, never
miss an opportunity. My plan is guaranteed and the
good thing about this plan is that if used intensely for
one year, the slaves themselves will remain perpetually
distrustful.[1]

This deeply disturbing illustration is, shamefully, part of our
nation's history and sadly true to our human nature. When the
focus is placed on accentuating differences in an unjust system of
reward and punishment driven by envy, fear, and distrust, there
can only be one outcome. For my black brothers and sisters, it

was servitude, submission, and bondage that were perpetuated for generations.

∾

When you and I buy into the same belief system and apply it to ourselves, the outcome is the same. When we focus on our faults, limitations, differences, and inner weaknesses, we reward ourselves with continual failure. There will always be someone taller, brighter, more gifted, more beautiful, more athletic, more . . . better . . . more . . . better . . . more . . . better.

We have a choice of masters. Will we serve the one who offers continual comparison with others of superior talent, position, and physical appearance? Or will we serve the one who designed us and placed himself within us?

> *Success is not measured*
> *by what you do compared to what others do;*
> *it is measured*
> *by what you do with the ability God gave you.*
>
> Zig Ziglar

What are your natural abilities? *Ability* can be defined as being able; the power to do something; skill, or talent. Natural abilities are the mental, social, emotional, and physical strengths passed on to us in our genetic makeup. They are the skills and talents that seem to appear from nowhere, as part of our standard equipment.

Bill Butterworth struggled to identify his real talents for many years because they were hidden in a short, pudgy body. When he changed his focus from competing on the athletic field to competing on the field of wit, wisdom, and speaking, he finally began to achieve and succeed.

Bill is a counselor, educator, author, and father of five who brings a refreshing perspective to the issue of abilities. Bill spoke for me at a leadership breakfast in the early nineties and shared some of his life with us.

He began by saying, "I weighed then what I weigh now, but I was twelve inches shorter and my last name was Butterworth—it wasn't a pretty picture."

In high school, athletes were rewarded with acceptance and friends. The football coach asked Bill if he would try out for the team, saying, "If we could just get you to hike the ball and fall over, no one would ever get to the quarterback and he'd complete every pass!" But Bill's mom would not allow her rotund son to participate in contact sports.

One day, his social studies teacher asked if he would consider going out for the track team. Bill thought, *Kids make fun of me all the time, and now the teachers are bringing me in for some one-on-one heckling.* But then someone encouraged Bill to try out for the shot put and the discus throw. He was told, "If you could ever get your beef behind that thing, you could really send it into orbit!" His mom agreed that it would be an opportunity for growth in self-esteem without the risk of punishing physical contact.

His self-esteem soared as he worked all winter in the gym, perfecting his style, his steps, and his shout as he released the imaginary objects indoors in anticipation of the spring track season. When the winter dream of success was awakened by the reality of actual performance, however, he failed badly. There was no winning shot toss or discus throw, just the unwelcome return of his old familiar friend: defeat.

One day, it appeared that he would be rescued by success on

the field of athleticism after all. His church was to participate
in an area-wide, all-church track competition. His teammate
Bobby, who was to run the 440-yard dash, was injured, and since
all other competitors were over their three-event limit, it was up
to Bill to run in his place.

> When you put on sprinter's spikes, something surreal
> happens. All the spikes are up front, and no matter how
> big you are—and I was the size of Utah—you feel fast
> . . . very fast! There was no time for strategy, so I took my
> starting assignment in lanes 4, 5, and 6. The gun went
> off and I heard my friends yelling, "It's only a lap," so I
> believed I could go all out from the start. At the 110-yard
> mark, I was neck and neck with the leader, running like a
> man possessed, while he paced himself for the rest of the
> race. At the 220-yard mark, I was in the lead, and it sud-
> denly dawned on me that I had been participating in the
> wrong events all this time! This was before *Chariots of Fire*
> or I'm sure an orchestra would have come up from the pit
> and I'd have started speaking Scottish!
>
> I was preparing my acceptance speech as I hit the
> 330-yard mark on the far side of the stadium. . . . And
> now I need to tell you the rest of the story as it was later
> told to me.
>
> The last thing I remember was the pain of sharp
> needles repeatedly injecting acid and Jell-O into my legs;
> everything was stinging and going soft. I fell to the track
> and into the path of the pounding footsteps of the run-
> ners behind, who proceeded to spike me beyond belief!
> I was ashamed to tell this story for years, until I realized
> that I had won the 330-yard dash!
>
> However, that wasn't the race I was supposed to run.[2]

Bill was never meant to compete with prowess on the athletic field—he never possessed the ability to succeed in that arena. But he did find success as a public speaker. In fact, he was the 1989 International Platform Speakers Association Speaker of the Year. He can now joke about those days of pain on the athletic fields because he moved on to pursue areas of life for which he was designed to succeed and win!

REFLECTIONS

Have you accepted yourself for who you are?

Whose standards are you trying to live up to? (Your peers? Your parents? The rich and famous? The athletic and beautiful? The majority?) If not theirs, then whose?

What would your life be like if you simply tried to follow the example of Jesus?

Do you believe God has given you a spiritual gift? What evidence of this gift is there in your life?

NUTS AND BOLTS

GETTING DOWN TO SPECIFICS

*God uniquely creates men (and women) for a
specific mission in life, and that assignment needs
to be identified and celebrated.*

—JOHN MAXWELL

WE ARE ALL surrounded by people of exceptional abilities.

I'm surrounded by three awesome women: Rita, Rebecca, and
Rachel. Rita has wonderful communication skills that allow her
to engage people, connect with them, and welcome them into
our home and into our lives. She stands all of four feet eleven
inches tall, weighs a mere one hundred–plus pounds, and has
blonde hair and blue eyes. She was the same twenty-five years
ago when we lived in inner-city Columbus and she worked with
African-American girls from the neighborhood. Her identity
in God and her understanding of her abilities reached across
ethnic and racial barriers and sustained her through burglary,

vandalism, and concerns for physical safety. She opened our home, made young girls feel welcome, and bridged the gap with a rightful confidence in her abilities.

Rebecca, our firstborn, takes initiative and has exceptional organization and networking abilities (not to mention a great sense of humor, poise, and style). She recently graduated from Ohio State University, with a degree in communications, and is pursuing a career in public relations built on her extensive background in athletics. During her four years at Ohio State, she served as a university host for the football team, worked in the compliance office, learning the ins and outs of college athletics, and took on several internships in marketing and public relations. That's a lot for anyone to achieve at any age, let alone by the time you're twenty-one!

Our younger daughter, Rachel, is very sensitive to people and to the environment around her. She is majoring in sociology at OSU, has worked in an after-school program with children at the Boys and Girls Clubs, and would one day like to counsel children and families. While the rest of the world sees snow falling, Rachel is able to see the single snowflake. Several years ago, we came out of a store on a snowy Saturday afternoon and headed to our van. Rachel said, "Look, Daddy!" Everyone else was rushing to wipe the snow off their cars, but Rachel was focused on a single, perfectly formed snowflake lying on the door handle of our red van. She sees, senses, and feels things that most of us miss.

What do you see that others miss? What are your abilities?

Arthur F. Miller and Ralph T. Mattson, authors of *The Truth About You,* offer valuable insights for self-discovery. Their research indicates that five ingredients are found in every person's makeup:

1. A central, driving motivation

2. A recurring way of operating with others

3. A distinct group of abilities

4. A recurring subject matter

5. Recurring circumstances

Miller and Mattson detail their findings as follows.[1] Where do you see yourself?

A CENTRAL MOTIVATION OF CRITICAL IMPORTANCE

Such motivations may be to acquire, be in charge, develop or build, discover or learn, excel, gain response, gain recognition, improve, master or perfect, overcome, pioneer or explore, serve or help, shape, influence, or control.

A RECURRING WAY OF OPERATING WITH OTHERS

- A *Team Member* wants to be with one other, or more.
- An *Individualist* wants to have his or her role defined and get results without relying on others.
- A *Team Leader* can lead others, but also wants to be involved in the action.
- A *Director* wants others to do things exactly as he or she wants them to be done.
- A *Coordinator* likes to be at the hub of the action and to plug in a variety of other people's efforts as they are needed.

- A *Coach* helps others to develop their talents or improve their knowledge.
- A *Manager* gets results by managing the talents of others.

A GROUP OF ABILITIES

- Administer/Maintain
- Analyze/Evaluate
- Build/Develop
- Control/Schedule
- Convince/Persuade
- Create/Shape
- Design/Draw
- Formulate/Theorize
- Do/Execute
- Innovate/Improvise
- Learn/Study
- Nurture/Nurse
- Make Friends/Build Relationships
- Operate/Run
- Organize/Plan
- Observe/Comprehend
- Perform/Entertain
- Teach/Train
- Practice/Perfect
- Research/Experiment
- Synthesize/Harmonize
- Write/Communicate

A Recurring Subject Matter

- Art/Design
- Concepts/Ideas
- Controls/Schedules/Budgets
- Details/Data
- Graphics
- Money
- Hardware/Equipment
- People/Relationships
- Systems
- Methods
- Technical/Mechanical Things
- Words/Language/Symbols

Recurring Circumstances

- Competition/Test
- Constraints/Deadlines
- Enterprise/Business
- Growth/Opportunity/Potential
- Needs/Causes
- New Situations
- Projects/Programs
- Stress Circumstances
- Structural Situations
- Trouble/Difficulty/Problems

If you were to thoughtfully review your life's experiences and achievements, you would identify a recurring motivation, ways of operating with others, and specific abilities, subject matter, and circumstances that have led to fulfilling achievements. That is your life pattern; it reveals what motivates and fulfills you, how you best relate to others, and what abilities are strongest.

You may want to stop and spend some time with this chart. I believe that the time you invest in it today will be rewarded a hundredfold or thousandfold tomorrow. It may be the doorway to a fulfilling future, or you may discover or affirm what already lies within you.

The life of one ordinary, everyday boy became a miracle once he discovered what was "already there."

> The first few times I looked down upon a human brain, or saw human hands working upon that center of intelligence and emotion and motion, working to help heal, I was hooked. Then, realizing that my hands were steady and that I could intuitively see the effect my hands had on the brain, I knew that I had found my calling. And so I made the choice that would become my career and my life.
>
> All the facets of my career came together. First, my interest in neurosurgery; second, my growing interest in the study of the brain; and third, acceptance of my God-given talent of eye-and-hand coordination—my gifted hands—that fitted me for this field. It seemed the most natural thing in the world.[2]

Dr. Benjamin Carson is a graduate of Yale University and the University of Michigan Medical School. He is currently the director of pediatric neurosurgery at Johns Hopkins University Hospital in Baltimore, Maryland. He is arguably the number one pediatric neurosurgeon in the world.

In 1987, Dr. Carson was on the seventy-member medical team that separated seven-month-old German twin boys. They were joined at the backs of their heads and shared the same major cerebral blood drainage system. In the twenty-two hour procedure, hypothermia—the deliberate lowering of body temperature—was coupled for the first time with circulatory bypass and deliberate cardiac arrest to spare brain tissue. The boys returned to Germany after seven months at Johns Hopkins.

Dr. Carson's efforts did not always lead to success. I spent two days with him in 1995 and learned a great deal more about him.

Ben and Curtis Carson had every reason to grow up angry. They were dirt poor, and their dad deserted them in childhood, leaving them to suffer the consequences of community violence, poverty, and a single-parent home in the slums of Detroit and Boston. Their mom, Sonya, worked two or three jobs as a domestic to meet their most basic needs and keep them off welfare. Ben was angry. One time, he nearly hit his mother with a hammer; another time, he assaulted a classmate with a combination lock and left him bloodied. The violence finally came to a head:

> The unthinkable happened. I lost control and tried to knife a friend. Bob and I were listening to a transistor radio when he flipped the dial to another station.
>
> "You call that music?" he demanded.

"It's better than what you like!" I yelled back, grabbing for the dial.

"Come on, Carson. You always. . . ."

In that instant, blind, pathological anger took possession of me. Grabbing the camping knife I carried in my back pocket, I snapped it open and lunged for the boy who had been my friend. With all the power of my young muscles, I thrust the knife toward his belly. The knife hit his heavy ROTC buckle with such force that the blade snapped and dropped to the ground.

I stared at the broken blade and went weak. I had almost killed my friend. If the buckle hadn't protected him, Bob would have been lying at my feet dying or severely wounded. I couldn't look him in the eye. Without a word, I turned and ran home.[3]

A mother who meant business turned this young boy around.

"Bennie," she said again and again, "if you can read, honey, you can learn just about anything you want to know. The doors of the world are open to people who can read. And my boys are going to be successful in life, because they're going to be the best readers in school."

As I think about it, I'm as convinced today as I was back in the fifth grade that my mother meant that. She believed in Curtis and me. She had such faith in us that we didn't dare fail! Her unbounded confidence nudged me into starting to believe in myself.

Several of Mother's friends criticized her strictness. I heard one woman ask, "What are you doing to those boys, making them study all the time? They're going to hate you."

"They can hate me," she answered, cutting off the woman's criticism, "but they're going to get a good education just the same!"[4]

Ben's mom believed in her boys. She instilled a strong faith in God in them. She made them go to the library and read and write a report on two books each week—even though she was unable to read. She kept this a secret from Ben and Curtis.

In the fifth grade, Ben believed that he was the dumbest kid in the class, and his grades proved it. Ben could tell you the make, model, year, and price of every car that passed on the street, but he couldn't read. As the saying goes, that knowledge and fifty cents could buy him a Coke at the corner store—but it prepared him for nothing in life. His mom turned off the TV and the radio and took her two boys to the "educational woodshed." In the seventh grade, the kids who used to make fun of him came to him for assistance with math homework.

In the eighth grade, Ben dreamed of being a surgeon.

In the ninth grade, his temper still needed taming, and he almost killed his friend.

That night, he picked up his Bible, talked to God, thought about everything his mother had been telling him, and embraced the fact that God, the one who created the universe, had also created him.

That night, Benjamin S. Carson allowed God to change him. "From age fourteen, I began to focus on the future. My mother's lessons were at last paying off."

Your story may not be as dramatic as Ben Carson's, but it's still your story. God created and equipped you with abilities that are to be developed and used.

What is your dream? What will you do to reach it?

ACTIONS

Using the information from this chapter, answer the following questions:

What is your primary or central motivation?

What is the most frequently recurring way you operate with others?

What are your top three groups of abilities?

What subject matter do you most prefer to work with?

What recurring circumstances do you most often operate in?

What is your primary spiritual gift?

What are three ways you will use your strengths and gifts in the week ahead?

Share this information with a trusted friend or mentor and ask him or her for any insights to help you fully operate in your areas of strength.

GOD EQUIPS
THE CHOSEN

PUTTING IT ALL TOGETHER

Now, with God's help, I shall become myself.

—SØREN KIERKEGAARD

I HAVE A friend whose life is marked by the spiritual gifts of leadership and giving. He's a humble, successful business person and a community leader who is generous with his wealth. His name is David R. Meuse.

David is the former chairman and CEO of Banc One Capital Holdings Corporation and is currently a principal with Stonehenge Partners, a highly successful Midwest private equity firm. In a time of national economic recession, his firm continues to outperform the vast majority of his competitors.

David will quickly tell you that the firm's success does not rest solely upon his ability to pick the right stocks or select the correct risk. His success has come from leading others and building the right team. He says, "Being a fully present leader, one who leads with values, intention, and purpose, takes a strong sense of self-awareness—including getting your ego out of the way—and knowing your strengths and weaknesses. A fully present leader lives and leads from the head, heart, and soul."[1]

The October 2004 edition of *Columbus CEO* magazine has a picture of David on the cover above the storyline, "Equity EMPIRE—How David Meuse and Stonehenge Partners Built an Investment Banking Powerhouse." The thoughts of one of his partners are reflected in the article:

> We have a team here that is an eclectic team. Everyone's background is just a little bit different. We're not just the right-down-the-middle-of-the-fairway group. And because of that, we have the opportunity to look at things a little differently and think outside the box.[2]

I believe that the bottom-line reason for the company's success is David's God-given leadership ability. He knows who he is, he has built a team, and he has kept his ego out of the office. He has identified people with differing abilities, skills, and knowledge, and molded them into a "band of brothers," as recognized in the inside article: "Band of Brothers—The high-octane team at Stonehenge Partners keeps racking up impressive investment returns. So why aren't they more . . . pompous?"

They aren't pompous because they follow David's leadership, and he has molded them through his personal character, natural abilities, and Spirit-given ability to lead. He is doing what comes naturally and what comes supernaturally, as well. David hates the things that God hates, and he acts upon his gifting with pure motives to build up those around him. From the abundance that David receives as a successful leader and businessman, he gives generously to the work of God in the world.

One of God's great beauties is that while he operates in the corporate boardroom, he also operates in the slums and asylums of the world. He seeks out and cares for the poor, the alienated, and the dying. He uses people with different gifts to care for others in different, but always redemptive, ways. We must never forget that God is everywhere.

Bono, the lead singer of U2, poignantly reminds us of this:

> God is in the slums, in the cardboard boxes where the poor play house. God is in the silence of a mother who has infected her child with a virus that will end both their lives. God is in the cries heard under the rubble of war. God is in the debris of wasted opportunity and lives and God is with us if we are with them.[3]

Where God is present with the poor and dying, he often enlists people with the gifts of helping. Helps can be defined as assisting leaders and meeting the needs of others in practical ways.

A young woman named Kirsta Niemie has the gift of helping. Here are some excerpts from an e-mail Kirsta sent to her family and friends when she was assisting in Mother Teresa's Home for the Dying in Calcutta, India. She lived there for months, away from family and friends, facing uncertainty, ethnic strife, and human fears. She was there to exercise her spiritual gift by helping others:

I have been learning that because God uses the least to do the most, this means I am a likely candidate to be used. I feel encouraged because I didn't feel worthy to be here doing this kind of work. . . .

I'm not a very "Holy" person and I'm not the most caring and I'm not the most selfless, but I was asked to come and depend on Jesus, he has been asking me to die to myself. . . .

I am sick right now. I have a horrible cold, stomach problems, a fever, lice, millions of mosquito bites, and so on. Through this time of constant physical discomfort I am asked to go outside myself and my ailments to love. . . .

It is easier and harder than I thought. Jesus helps me every day, but it is still a challenge. . . .

Yesterday I went to Kalighat and the woman I had been taking care of, Batima, died. I knew she was close the other day because she was slipping in and out of consciousness so I sat next to her bed and prayed over her . . .

I didn't quite know how to feel . . . it was expected, but I am still very sad. I realized I may be the only person in the world besides Jesus that cares she is dead, that mourned her death, that will miss her presence.[4]

The beauty of this e-mail comes in Kirsta's awareness that she's not the most gifted or most caring person, but that she is still willing to meet the needs of others in practical ways. In helping and serving, she reached new depths in her relationship with God that came only as she emptied herself of "self" and exercised her spiritual gift. In spite of her sickness and the misery around her, she found fulfillment in using what God has placed within her.

∾

These few concrete examples of how gifts and abilities are being used for others encourage each of us to examine our abilities and our gifting and ask God what he wants us to do with our lives.

You already know my bias. I believe that he is calling us to redemptive action. He is asking us to set others free so that they can be restored to God. He is asking us to use what he has given us. What does that mean to you? What will your life of redemptive action look like?

You and I are not alone. At the 2006 White House National Conference on Faith-Based and Community Initiatives, President George W. Bush said, "America is witnessing a quiet transformation, a revolution of conscience, in which a rising generation is finding that a life of personal responsibility is a life of fulfillment."[5]

What will you do?

There are many challenges ahead for you and for our country. We live in a sex-crazed society. Too often, the poor have no voice, and the innocent pay the price for the guilty. Many religious, business, civic, and government leaders seem attracted only to corruption. Genuine faith is increasingly marginalized, and as a nation, we kill 1.5 million unborn babies every year.

I see a world in which there is an adult problem, not a youth problem. Adults produce illegal drugs, distribute pornography, lie, and break life commitments.

We're surrounded by "reality TV." As a culture, we are consumed with interest in billionaires with bad hair and TV programs that reward selfishness. We have elevated the phrase "you're fired!" to an almost religious status. We have women in sports bras and tight shorts entertaining viewers with outrageous stunts and gross challenges under the title of *Fear Factor*.

On TV, we also "trade spouses" with overbearing, domineering, anorexic, or obese women and place them cross-culturally in homes with disconnected husbands and fathers to reward the very worst behavior. For relief from this insanity we can, of course, turn to *The Man Show* or *Desperate Housewives.*

The local news tries to scare you enough at 6:00 P.M. to make you tune in at 11:00 P.M. to watch the latest consumer scare or crime story. Our national news programs often create the news instead of reporting it. The conservative Right affirms truth, but too often communicates its message in abusive and arrogant terms. The liberal Left too often condescendingly ignores the truth. Both distort the facts.

Of the 163 democracies on the planet today, America ranks 140th in voter turnout, and yet we champion democracy to the world.[6] Lost and lonely people tune in to religious TV programs and find sweaty ministers in $3,000 suits proclaiming, "Name it and claim it," "Blab it and grab it," or "Touch the TV and you'll be healed!"

I fuel my car at the local gas station and shake my head as a young man drives away from the pump with a plastic Jesus and a radar detector on his dashboard.

When I visit a student dorm at a major university, I'm welcomed by two signs as I approach the information desk: *Getting Any Nookie?* and *Cookies and Condoms—Tuesday night, 7:00 p.m. in Room 200.* You bet, a "condom social" so that each sexually hungry, hormonally driven young adult can load up on the latex solution to birth control. I read the paper and see that the murder of a black teenager from the hood is buried on page 18, whereas the murder of a pretty suburban girl is front-page news.

It's disturbing, and it's real. I didn't make this stuff up.

What will you do to change it in some small way?

What will you pass on to the generation that will step into your footprints?

Isn't it your responsibility to leave this world a better place when you depart?

Are you willing to pray and do, love and touch, risk and trust?

We need to become God's agents of change, or get another god.

Perhaps you are the person who will start a movement that severely restricts or ends partial-birth abortion, abortion, or pornography. You may turn the tide in holding our political leaders accountable for their words and actions. You could restore hope, health, and economic prosperity to an inner-city neighborhood. You might influence the world of media . . . education . . . race relations . . . poverty . . .

Maybe God wants you to be the one person who cares for the elderly woman or the lonely single that lives unnoticed around the corner or just up the street.

Yes, many aspects of our culture are disturbing, but if we are not bothered by the problems, we're contributing to them. If we are not in some small way committed to changing it, then we are not loving God or loving others as ourselves.

God designed and created you for this day, for this moment. As he reminds each of us, "I have engraved you on the palms of my hands" (Isaiah 49:16). In Hebrews 2:6-8, the author addresses God, asking, "What is man that you are mindful of him, the son of man that you care for him? You made him a little lower than the angels; you crowned him with glory and honor and put everything under his feet."

These passages reveal the source of our hope. We don't do this alone. What God calls you to do, he equips you to accomplish.

ACTIONS

Write down your answers to the following questions:

What are the three most important relationships in your life?

Why do you believe you will spend eternity with God?

Pray and ask Jesus to change your life.

FRIENDSHIP WITH GOD

LIVING THE FIRST SACRED PRIORITY

*You have made us for yourself, O God, and the
heart of man is restless until it finds rest in you.*

—Saint Augustine

By AGE TWENTY, he was a millionaire two and a half times over.
His travels took him from his wealthy family in Westchester
County, New York, to a private Catholic school, a men's finishing school in Europe, to all fifty states and twenty-six countries
around the world. At age sixteen, he was a copilot for Pan Am; at
age eighteen, he was chief resident pediatrician for a hospital in
Georgia; at age nineteen, he passed the Louisiana bar exam and
accepted a position as assistant attorney general, and at twenty, he
was a professor at Brigham Young University in Provo, Utah.

He started all this with a tenth-grade education and $200 in his checking account.

If ever a young man succeeded in storing up wealth, position, possessions, pleasures, and fame for himself, it was Frank W. Abagnale Jr.

Frank Abagnale was Frank Abagnale's number one priority, and he valued money, freedom, independence, travel, and recognition. He built all of this on the foundation of a remarkably seamless deception. He was also a sixteen-year-old kid on the run, seeking to fill the void in his life brought on by his parents' divorce. When he left home, he found himself working for $1.25 an hour.

That was about to change.

He would soon be known as "the great imposter," "the skyway man," and "the world's greatest con man." He had an IQ of 140; he was six feet tall, and he was prematurely gray around the temples. In a suit, he looked ten years older than he was. He had a commanding presence, and bank after bank was pleased to cash his bad checks.

He purchased a Pan Am copilot's uniform for $286, secured a fraudulent ID card, and flew three million miles as a "guest" of the airline. As a copilot, he had the privilege of flying with any airline in the cockpit jump seat. City to city, state to state, and country to country, he ate airline food, stayed in airline housing, and wrote hundreds of thousands of dollars in bad checks. He was never detained in his life of crime. Former FBI agent Joseph Shea once commented, "He was very good at being very bad at a very young age."[1]

Frank left Pan Am at age eighteen to settle in Atlanta, Georgia. He passed himself off as Dr. Frank Williams, a pediatrician on sabbatical from his practice in California. Unfortunately, one of his neighbors was a physician. In order to maintain his front, he was soon spending six hours each day reading the latest medical journals at Emory University so that he could speak knowledgeably about medical matters.

It worked. He was soon approached by his friend, who needed to fill a midnight to 8:00 A.M. shift at a new hospital with a resident pediatrician supervisor. He took a tour of the hospital, met the staff, and was pleased to say that because he was not licensed in Georgia, he could not accept the job.

In Georgia at that time, a physician only needed to pass an oral exam to receive certification. He passed the exam and found himself scribbling on charts, but never once did he examine, diagnose, treat, or administer drugs. The residents loved him, because he allowed them to do all the work!

A former chief of police of Houston, Texas, said, "Frank Abagnale could write a check on toilet paper, drawn on the Confederate States treasury, sign it 'U.R. Hooked' and cash it at any bank in town using a Hong Kong driver's license for identification."[2] Obviously, he was indeed "very good at being very bad at a very young age."

A year later, Abagnale moved to Baton Rouge, Louisiana, where he took the name Bob Conrad and posed as a highly successful attorney. It wasn't long before he met the state attorney general. You guessed it—on his third try, he passed the bar exam and accepted a position as assistant attorney general for the state of Louisiana.

At each step in his life of deception and crime, he utilized his wit, his commanding physical features, and his intelligence to take advantage of others. While visiting a bank on one occasion, he took home a stack of blank deposit slips, professionally imprinted his own checking account number on each of them, replaced them on the counter the next day, and returned later to withdraw the $40,000 that others had unknowingly deposited into his account in just six hours!

Another time, while flying the friendly skies, he noticed that many of the airport shops deposited their money into a secure night deposit box at the end of the evening shift. He showed up the next night with the appropriate security company uniform, hung an Out of Order sign over the deposit box, and kindly accepted all of the day's receipts onto his dolly, which he wheeled off to the privacy of his room.

On numerous occasions, he cashed personal checks—never more than $100—at each of the airline counters at major airports around the world. He soon discovered that if he took his time and cashed $100 checks at each airline, it would take him approximately eight hours to cover the entire airport.

At the end of eight hours of work, just about anywhere in the world, a new shift comes on. Frank would make the rounds one more time, walking away with thousands of dollars in cash for his efforts. At the height of his fraud, at nineteen years of age, he rode in a chauffeur-driven Rolls Royce and stayed in $600 per day hotel rooms. This lifestyle cost him $50,000 a month.

He was caught in France at age twenty-one when an Air France flight attendant identified him. He was convicted and imprisoned nude for six months in solitary confinement. His six-foot frame was squeezed into a five-by-five-by-five foot cell, with a daily diet of soup, coffee, bread, and water. He had to sleep sitting up to avoid suffocating in the urine and excrement that filled his cell.

He had wasted away from 200 pounds to 109 pounds when he was released, first to Sweden, and then on to confinement with a ten-year sentence in the Atlanta Federal Prison. Since its construction in 1902, there had never been an escape there, but thirteen days after his incarceration, Frank walked out the front door of the prison, impersonating a federal prison inspector. He was captured again and spent four years in a federal prison in

Virginia before he was paroled in 1974 to assist the federal government in developing anti-fraud systems.[3]

ॐ

Frank Abagnale's story recently played on the big screen in the Hollywood production of *Catch Me If You Can,* starring Leonardo DiCaprio as Frank. The movie gives him a platform for speaking about his new priorities in life—priorities that transcend personal gain and selfish consumption.

Since his release from prison, Frank Abagnale has made a dramatic turnaround in his life. He now says that he wasted his entire youth and much of his life. He has repented of his illegal actions and has made full restitution of the $2.5 million he took from his victims. He developed an anti-fraud consulting firm in Tulsa, Oklahoma that serves the world's largest banks, hotels, retail companies, the FBI, and government agencies around the world. He has gone from being the most notorious fraud in the world to helping establish international security systems to deter fraud and capture criminals who are intent upon defrauding others of their capital resources. He has achieved the same measure of success as a millionaire on the right side of the law as he did when he was using others to feed his selfish desires for money, pleasure, and position. Frank said, "I have been married for over twenty-five years and I am the proud father of three sons. Age brings wisdom, and fatherhood changes one's life completely. I regard my past as immoral, unethical, and illegal. It is not something that I am proud of. I am proud that I have been able to turn my life around, and in the past twenty-five years, I have helped my government, my clients, and thousands of corporations and consumers to deal with the problems of white-collar crime and fraud."[4]

Frank realized that he could live as a free man only when he placed the needs of others above his own; he came to believe that something existed outside of himself that was more important than he was. He discovered this in family life and in helping others.

○∿

What priorities guide your life?

Does something exist beyond you that gives your life value and meaning?

What ultimate truth do you hold sacred?

God is the ultimate truth, and I believe that deep down, you want to please him. When you do so, you express your priorities and reveal the truths that you hold most sacred; the ones that guide your life. I regard these sacred priorities as the important areas in your life—the ones that take precedence over all others, and that have been dedicated to God and set apart for his purposes in you and in the world.[5]

Four priorities give meaning to my life. They provide a lens through which I view the world, a path upon which my feet travel, and a rudder that holds me on course during the difficult storms of life. They are truthful, so they guide me through life's big issues as I negotiate the smaller details. Larry Kreider, president of The Gathering/USA, often reminds me that "priorities are like the rudder of a sailing vessel. Though the ship is large and driven by strong winds, the rudder guides the ship to its destination." What guides you to your destination?

My first sacred priority is my relationship with God.

This relationship began when I was a teen, and it continues to grow, change, and deepen as I mature. I have tested it against many other "realities" and many other "truths," and I have come back every time to the realization that Jesus is the doorway to God.

My relationship with God is personal. It is dynamic, so it grows and changes over time. It requires a commitment that must be renewed daily—giving all that I know about myself to all that I know about God on this particular day.

Jesus is the most important part of priority one.

When I look at what all the great leaders of mankind have said, done, and stood for, I find that one man has distinguished himself above all others. Jesus of Nazareth, the son of Joseph and Mary, is the Son of God, who lived among us and showed us the way to God. He left behind a way of life that gives me life. He left behind an empty tomb.

Jesus never said that I had to be better or more religious than the next guy. He never said that I had to be perfect. He simply said, "Come, follow me." I never needed anyone to tell me that I fell short of God's standard—my heart told me that all along.

I knew that I needed God's grace to enter heaven and that I could never get there on my own.

I believe that God is the Supreme Being over all of humanity: prostitutes, politicians, CEOs, salesmen, domestics, illegal aliens, soccer moms, and rock stars. He knows how each of us can best relate to him. He has pointed out our weaknesses and wrongdoings, and he has provided a way for us to be reconciled through the grace of his Son, Jesus. Bono drives this point home:

> I love the idea that God says: Look, you cretins, there are
> certain results to the way we are, to selfishness, and there's
> mortality as part of your very sinful nature, and, let's face
> it, you're not living a very good life, are you? There are
> consequences to actions. The point of the death of Christ

is that Christ took on the sins of the world, so that what we put out did not come back to us, and that our sinful nature does not reap the obvious death. That's the point. It should keep us humble. It's not our own good works that get us through the gates of heaven.[6]

I would never call you a cretin, but I know that I'm the selfish mortal that Bono is speaking about. I'm humbled to know that there is a God who loves me and who offers to do for me what I cannot do for myself.

I'm humbled that God would sacrifice his Son for me. "God so loved the world that he gave his one and only Son, that whoever believes in him shall not perish but have eternal life" (John 3:16). It's our choice, yours and mine, to accept or reject this reality. When I encountered Jesus, the burden of guilt and remorse was taken from my shoulders. I discovered that God did not slap me down; he embraced me.

The hole in my heart was filled.

I'm humbled that God would offer me life when I've failed him so often. "For the wages of sin is death, but the gift of God is eternal life in Christ Jesus our Lord" (Romans 6:23). When I admitted that I fell short of God's standard of perfection and that sin was a very real part of my life, I could accept God's gift.

I got much more than a hot-air balloon ride out of hell. I get to know God, hear his voice, and live in an indescribable relationship with my Creator. He is with me every day. He's not my "Cosmic Problem Solver" or my "Get Me out of This Situation Genie." He is my Father and my Friend.

What else would I ever want him to be?

God designed and created us to live in a vitally fulfilling relationship with him and with our fellow humans. Our relationships have been corrupted by sin. God sent Jesus to die in payment for the sins of humanity. Only as we profess faith in Jesus, accept his death on the cross, and receive his forgiveness can we be restored to our originally intended relationships.

Where do you stand today in relation to Jesus?

I believe we come to him in different ways, times, and seasons of our lives. There is no "one size fits all" pathway to Jesus. Some come as children, some as adults, and some on their deathbeds. Some come from a background of pristine beauty and success, and some come by way of the gutter. Jesus offers us life, and we offer our lives in return, just like Rachel Scott, Chris Spielman, Maximilian Kolbe—and even Johnny Cash.

Johnny Cash lived a life of dark success. I say *dark* because he was prone to disturbing thoughts, depression, alcohol abuse, and illegal drug use. At his lowest point, he crawled into a cave, filled himself with drugs and alcohol, and lay down to die. When he awoke, the light he saw was not the light of eternity. It was the dimly filtering light reflecting into the cave where he lay on the cold, hard earth. When he crawled out, he stepped into a new life of hope and faith guided by a relationship with Jesus.

Johnny Cash's life and music reflected the change, and he suffered with poor record sales as the result. But for him it was well worth the penalty. He once wrote, "To be practical about it, you have to admit that if you were in my shoes and believed what I believe, you'd have been a fool to choose a decade or two's worth of record sales over eternal salvation."[7]

Do you recognize Jesus of Nazareth as the Son of God, who was sent in love to show us the way to forgiveness, peace, and fulfillment? What have you offered to Jesus for what he has offered to you?

Have you made a personal commitment to him as Lord, Lover, Master, Messiah, Savior, Leader, Boss, and CEO of your life?

If not, why not ask him to forgive your sins and make you complete?

He will bring you peace beyond understanding, give you wisdom to make sense of our troubling world, and take you home to be with him forever. Since this priority is so important to me, I want to explore it more deeply. I believe that your commitment to Jesus takes priority over all others.

Bobby Bowden is the head football coach at Florida State University and the winningest gridiron coach in Division I collegiate history. Coach Bowden joined two-time Heisman Trophy Award–winner Archie Griffin in Columbus a few years ago for a breakfast event and shared the following story with our audience.

He was an outstanding college baseball player, but he was definitely not known for his home-run power. In 1951, he had the perfect hit at the perfect time and drove the ball between the shortstop and second baseman and between the centerfielder and leftfielder. The ball rolled all the way to the wall. He rounded first, headed toward second, and was still churning toward third when he saw his coach waving him home.

The catcher was waiting for him in the base path, squatting to receive the throw from the outfield and tag out the speedy Bowden. The ball arrived a split second before Bobby hit the catcher with the full force of his small body. As the ball squirted away from his mitt, the umpire called Bowden safe with an inside-the-park home run! While he and the team celebrated his first-ever home run, the catcher picked up the loose ball and threw it to the first baseman, who stepped on the bag as the umpire called him out! How was this possible?

Bobby recalls, "I remember rounding first and touching second and third, but I can't quite remember touching first base." Bobby didn't touch first and was declared out. It didn't matter that he touched second, third, and home, because without touching first base, all the subsequent bases were ruled null and void. So it is with Jesus. If he does not become your first priority in life, it really doesn't matter how many people you help, how much money you give away, or how often you go to church. Jesus is the key to all that follows. He is the first base in life that validates your journey to second, third, and home. He says, "I am the way and the truth and the life. No one comes to the Father except through me" (John 14:6).

Jesus does not play favorites. He offers his grace to all people, everywhere, at all times. A number of years ago, Coach Bowden attended a church service with his wife and children and noticed that he and his wife were "bookends" to their six kids, who were spread out across the front row. To illustrate faith, the minister asked Bowden if he would walk across a beam twelve inches wide, twelve inches above the ground, and forty feet long for twenty dollars. Bobby assured him that he could and would.

The minister then upped the ante, "What if I placed that beam 110 stories high and hung it between two skyscrapers. Would you walk across it for $1 million?"

"Absolutely not," Bobby responded.

"Why not?" asked the minister.

Bobby responded, "I'm sure I would fall to my death. I don't believe that I would have the faith in myself to make it."

Once again the pastor upped the ante. "If I were to hold one of your children from the top of a building and threaten to drop him if you didn't walk the beam, what would you do then?"

Bobby looked down the aisle at each of his kids, thought for a minute, and said, "Which one?"

We smile, because we play favorites even with the people we love. With Jesus, there is no standard of behavior that we must reach before we become eligible for his grace. He walked the beam 110 stories up for each of us—for those we think of as holy and for those we know to be evil. He gave no second thought to the worthiness of those he came to die for.

Jesus' forgiveness erases our sins but not their consequences. We cannot see Jesus, but our faith is carried forward by hope in our Creator. It is also comprised of everyday, real-life components, such as living with the consequences of our actions even though our behaviors have been forgiven and forgotten.

Bobby tells a story about a farmer and his young son. Every time the boy did something wrong, his dad drove a nail into the barn door with his hammer. During the boy's teen years, the door became full of nails as the boy's life was characterized by misbehavior and misdeeds. Late in his teens, the boy came to faith in Jesus. In celebration of his son's commitment, the dad went out to the barn and pulled every nail from the door.

The son saw that the nails were gone, but the holes remained. He asked, "How do you get rid of the holes?"

His father replied, "You can't. You can get rid of the nails, but the scars remain."[8]

God's grace and forgiveness remove our guilt, but he doesn't necessarily change our circumstances; the holes remain when the nails are removed. The loss of a child, AIDS, divorce, bankruptcy, desertion, or betrayal may all be consequences of sin in our lives. None of these will disappear, and none of them can separate you from God's love. God will use your losses to enable you to better love and serve others. God even uses the holes that remain in our lives. That is a miracle!

THE NEXT SACRED PRIORITIES

LOVING OUR NEIGHBORS AS OURSELVES

What good is it, my brothers, if a man claims to have
faith but has no deeds? Can such faith save him?
Suppose a brother or sister is without clothes and daily
food. If one of you says to him, "Go, I wish you well;
keep warm and well fed," but does nothing about his
physical needs, what good is it? In the same way, faith
by itself, if it is not accompanied by action, is dead.

—JAMES 2:14–17

EACH OF MY priorities comes directly from the words of Jesus found in Matthew 22:37, 39. He said, "Love the Lord your God with all your heart and with all your soul and with all your mind." And, "Love your neighbor as yourself."

Jesus taught that all priorities and purposes are tied to loving

God and loving your neighbor. If you and I follow Jesus in just these two things, we will have every other priority in order.

But don't miss what Jesus says there at the end: "Love your neighbor *as yourself.*" This tells me something exceedingly important for my well-being. It tells me that not only is it *okay* to love myself, it tells me that it's . . . *expected.*

My second sacred priority is a personal and progressive commitment to loving myself.

Please stay with me on this one. This is not a call to self-centeredness, but to seeing ourselves as God sees us. We follow Jesus' example in personal development, growth, and maturity. The more we develop, the more we can give to God and the more he can do through us.

I love what the Bible says in Ephesians 2:10: "We are God's workmanship, created in Christ Jesus to do good works, which God prepared in advance for us to do." Our self-concept depends to a large degree upon what we think the most important person in our life thinks about us. If that person is Jesus, we will have a clear model for a healthy identity.

Dr. John Tolson, founder of The Gathering/USA, once told me, "As long as you live, you learn; and as long as you learn, you live." He believes that the investment we make in ourselves to continually grow and mature enables us to get the most out of life and give the most to others. This is why it is so important to know and understand our gifts, abilities, mission, purpose, and passions in life. The better we understand ourselves and develop our potential, the better we can serve others. We can make more of a difference in our world through the transforming power of redemptive action.

When I invest in myself, I live a balanced, God-centered life. Comedian and youth expert Ken Davis says that the balanced life is "characterized by order, peace, and wholeness."[1] Isn't that what we all want?

When Jesus is at my center, he helps me hold all of the competing demands of my life in a healthy, dynamic, and fruitful tension that results in order, peace, and wholeness. This allows me to say yes to some things and requires that I say no to others. I must base such decisions upon my priorities.

When I spend time with God, love my wife and daughters, and give myself to exercise, work, study, play, relationships, church, and community commitments, I find that my life is in balance. The "wheel of my life" may not be a perfect circle, but if I'm centered on God, he helps me stay on track.

Relax, take a deep breath, enjoy the journey, and exercise some personal discipline, remembering that God expects progress, not perfection. It is our responsibility to manage the competing demands of our lives by being aware of our priorities. When our priorities are in line, the time factor will take care of itself.

When I find myself out of balance, I'm reminded of my commitment to focus on the pure and the eternal: "Whatever is true, whatever is noble, whatever is right, whatever is pure, whatever is lovely, whatever is admirable—if anything is excellent or praiseworthy—think about such things" (Philippians 4:8). We begin to grow and achieve the balance we desire when we recognize God as the source of all we possess, focus our thoughts and motivations on giving life to others, and honor our human limitations.

I don't believe that God calls us to a 24/7/365 rat race of hurry, worry, and strain.

⚬⚬

My third sacred priority is to live in significant relationships with others.

I give priority to relationships with my wife, family, and friends, and my community of fellow followers of Jesus. Other relationships are of value to me, but my closest relationships head the list. I continue to learn much from others about the sacred priority of relationships, especially in my family.

I learned something about family while sitting in the surgical-unit waiting room at Shands Hospital in Gainesville, Florida, as doctors removed cancerous breast tissue from my sister-in-law, Cindy. She was surrounded by family members who cried, expressed their love, hugged, showed affection, and showered her with prayer and blessings.

There can be no compromise with family. Family love is not a matter of convenience, but of commitment. My father-in-law, John Toth, models this commitment well. For the past twelve years, he has gently, diligently, and humbly cared for his wife, Irene, who is stricken with advanced Alzheimer's disease. He feeds, bathes, and clothes her, washes and styles her hair, trims her nails, puts her to bed, takes her to the toilet, talks to her, kisses her, and prays and hopes for her. She will not be removed from their home and placed in a treatment facility as long as John is there and family is close by. That is family love.

Six hours later, we remained in the hospital waiting room, waiting to visit with Cindy, who had come through her surgery remarkably well. Meanwhile, something amazing was happening. The many families in the waiting area had become one large family. We had begun to care for one another. We were learning names, getting acquainted, sharing our burdens and resources, and lightening the load for one another. We were becoming a community.

The hospital staff had left the waiting area for the day, but all the family members who were still waiting were manning the phones and taking calls as the patients came down from surgery. We each had something to give to the others, and we each received something that we needed. A hard-of-hearing "good ol' boy" from south Georgia was updating families on their loved ones. Rita spoke with a mom who was awaiting word on her son, who had been in a terrible car accident. We created community in a hospital waiting room and discovered that God was in our midst.

God designed humanity to live in community in order to help and love each other. Community consists of relationships, so relationships are a high priority for me. Jesus modeled this type of community when he was on earth by connecting with people in such a way that they became committed to him and to one another. They looked first to the needs of others before their own. They chose the common good as a higher priority than individual achievement. On occasion, they sold what they had and shared it with others in need. That is what I mean by community, and that is what I believe God is asking of us today in our churches and houses of worship.

Dr. Jay Kesler, my former boss and a past president of Taylor University, underscores the value of community when he writes, "The Church of Jesus Christ was begun by Christ and is the one institution that He holds dearest to His heart. . . . In the New Testament, there is nothing taught about individual wholeness in the modern sense of the term—that is, that man is autonomous and self-contained. When we have wholeness in Christ, there is a body wholeness whereby the body is made complete by the complementary gifts that God has given each of His children."[2]

In other words, there are no lone rangers in God's family. We live in community to give and receive, not as spectators, but as participants, for our benefit and for that of our brothers and sisters.

For the past eighteen years, I've begun nearly every Thursday morning with a small group of ten men. We listen to, share with, and pray for one another, and seek to better know and understand God by studying Scripture. We care for one another through the loss of jobs, parents, and loved ones, and we support each other when going through difficult personal times. Sometimes my day is made complete just by being with these men. God desires this strength of community for each of us. It continues what Jesus did with his inner circle of followers.

My fourth and final sacred priority is a personal, dynamic commitment to the world around me.

This priority really goes back to the underlying theme of my life—the call to redemptive action. My life becomes whole as I daily touch others' lives as a bridge that will restore them to God and to their world. I recognize what God has done for me, and I follow Jesus' example.

The most exciting thing about this priority is that I don't have to sign up as a volunteer in order to have an impact on my world. I don't need an organization, a cause, or a predetermined outcome. I don't have to go somewhere else to accomplish it, after first completing an application and a training course.

We Americans love to organize goodness and compassion, and there is nothing wrong with that. In fact, it's something I've done most of my life. My point is that as we encounter life with its people, problems, and possibilities, we have many opportunities to respond in simple or profound ways.

Certain demands are placed upon us if we are to act redemptively. We must show up for life with an awareness of others and their needs. We must also subject our selective judgments and criticisms to God's ultimate truth: God is love. How we respond to this truth determines everything!

Let me illustrate this by taking a page from Jesus' life.

On one occasion, the local religious leaders brought a woman to him who had been caught in adultery. They quoted the law of Moses to Jesus, insisting that she be stoned to death. They asked Jesus what he would do with her. He ignored their question and began to write with his finger in the sand. Perhaps he listed the sins of each accuser.

Please note two things here. First, the accusers did not bring in the man, who was also guilty of adultery. Where was he? Didn't he sin? Second, the witness to the act of adultery was supposed to pick up the first stone to begin the stoning. Why didn't he step forward with a stone in his hand? The religious leaders apparently made selective judgments. They hypocritically condemned one party to the adultery while allowing the other to go free.

When the religious leaders continued to pound Jesus with questions about the woman, he said, "If any one of you is without sin, let him be the first to throw a stone at her." He then bent down and continued to write in the sand. The men walked away one by one, leaving Jesus and the woman alone. With no one left to condemn her, Jesus extended God's highest, truest law of love to her, saying, "Neither do I condemn you. Go now and leave your life of sin" (John 8:7, 11).

Before we close this section, I'd like to mention two additional insights.

First, Jesus pointed out the religious leaders' "selective justice," and faced with that, they walked away. Second, Jesus did not let the woman off the hook. He did not condemn her to death by stoning, but he told her to go and sin no more. In other words, he told her to leave her lifestyle of sin and get a new life, which is essentially the same message he gave the religious leaders.

Jesus placed constraints on the actions of the religious leaders and of the woman. Jesus did not condemn her, but he let her know that God's love required a different lifestyle from her in the future. When we look at this story, we often see the need for the men to change, and fail to see that the woman was required to change as well. When we act redemptively in our world, people are moved to make changes.

∾

"Pistol Pete" Maravich was a college basketball All-American and an NBA All-Star. He died in his early forties while playing the game he loved. In 1986, while Pete was waiting for friends to complete a six-mile race, he saw a young Hispanic boy pushing the wheelchair of a young black boy with no arms or legs. These competitors became very special to Pete as he watched.

Five hundred yards from the finish line, the Hispanic boy stopped, picked up his black friend from the wheel chair and carried him 400 yards closer to the line. He then placed him on the ground and lay beside him in the dust as they crawled to the finish line together.[3]

If you are the young black boy on the ground, God is there beside you all the way, lovingly caring for you regardless of your state in life. If you are the Hispanic boy, you are the hands and feet of God, expressing his love and nurtured by the relationships of others. God the Father watches you from above, Jesus the Son crawls beside you in the dust, the Holy Spirit lives within you, and the community of believers is all around you.

You are never alone.

God called you to make a difference in the lives of others and has equipped you with everything you need if you have Jesus in your life.

I have shared about my own life with Jesus, but I know nothing about your relationship with God. If you are looking for a relationship with him that you don't currently have, I invite you to pray with me and invite Jesus into your life as your difference maker and the lover of your soul.

If you want to do this, please pray the following with me: "God, thank you for loving me. Thank you for sending your Son to die on the cross for me. I am a sinner in need of your forgiveness. Please forgive me. I yield myself to you in accepting Jesus Christ as my Savior and Lord and ask you to fill me with your Holy Spirit. I commit myself to you today and ask for your grace to guide me every day for the rest of my life. Thank you for adopting me into your family. In Jesus' name, Amen."

Your life as a follower of Jesus Christ will be dynamic, growing, challenging, and hopeful. He will meet your deepest needs, fulfill your deepest desires, and give you life to the fullest. If you just prayed to receive Christ as your Savior, I would love to hear from you. Please send me an e-mail through my Web site: www.GatheringColumbus.com.

If you want to go deeper in your relationship with God, I recommend that you pick up a copy of *The Four Priorities: Life's Too Short to Get It Wrong.* You can purchase a copy through The Gathering's Web site: www.TheGathering.org.

God bless you.

REFLECTIONS

What makes your top priorities superior to all others?

How does God influence your priorities?

WITHOUT COMPROMISE

HONORING JESUS' THREE CORE VALUES

God in his wisdom has ordained that man should ally himself absolutely to the Absolute, and only relatively to the relative.

But man in his finite wisdom has rather allied himself only relatively to the Absolute, and absolutely to that which is relative.

—SØREN KIERKEGAARD

GOD CALLS EACH of us to leave the world of the mediocre and the relative to pursue the excellent and the absolute. The core values that guide our lives and direct our choices determine our success as we align ourselves with God. We never compromise those values because they are more important than life.

Core values are the essence of what we determine is most important in life, or those things that we give worth to above all others. Many of Jesus' life experiences give us insight into his purpose, goals, priorities, and values. Jesus was often in conflict with the religious and political rulers of the day. On more than one occasion, Jesus disappeared into the hills because his faith, lifestyle, and relationships were so at odds with the values of others that they sought to take his life.

Jesus radically divided whatever community he entered. For some, he was the Christ, Messiah, Lord, Savior, Master, and King of kings. To others, he was a liar, lunatic, glutton, drunkard, rebel, radical, and sinner. Someone once said that Jesus is the great divider of life; you must walk parallel to him or directly cross his path. Jesus calls us to a radical commitment to him, and if we are to walk with him, we must understand the values he holds dear.

Jesus' values separated him from the crowd and distinguished him from the commonplace. They charted the course of his life and were integral to the impact he had on the world. They may do the same for you.

Jesus placed a high value on his faith as he worshiped and was submissive to God the Father. He placed great value on his lifestyle, the manner in which he lived out his faith. He interacted with individual people, regardless of their background.

Jesus had a fundamental faith, an evangelical lifestyle, and liberal relationships.

Depending upon your religious or political leanings, these terms may carry negative baggage for you. You may be passionately positive or negative about them, but it is important to understanding their root meanings and their proper application.

A fundamentalist accepts the Bible as the authoritative, infallible, divinely inspired Word of God and lives his or her life in accordance with its teachings. It's that simple. It really means getting down to basics in our faith. It has nothing to do with bombing abortion clinics or hating gays.

The word *evangel* means "good news" or "gospel." It's the root word for *evangelical.* Evangelicals believe that—as the Bible says—people come to faith in God through belief in Jesus. They recognize the authority of Scripture and the importance of telling others about Jesus.

A liberal person is generous and openhanded, an ample giver who is tolerant and free of authoritarianism and traditional forms. Thus defined, a liberal person is not inherently lacking in moral restraint or convention, but rather is generous with his time and resources and understands the weaknesses of others.

Let me tie all of this together by looking briefly at one experience from Jesus' life that provides a deeper understanding of these three values.

> Jesus stepped into a boat, crossed over and came to his own town. Some men brought to him a paralytic, lying on a mat. When Jesus saw their faith, he said to the paralytic, "Take heart, son; your sins are forgiven." At this, some of the teachers of the law said to themselves, "This fellow is blaspheming!" Knowing their thoughts, Jesus said, "Why do you entertain evil thoughts in your hearts? Which is easier: to say, 'Your sins are forgiven,' or to say, 'Get up and walk'? But so that you may know that the Son of Man has authority on earth to forgive sins . . ." Then he said to the paralytic, "Get up, take your mat and go home." And the man got up and went home. When the crowd saw this, they were filled with awe; and they praised God, who had given such authority to men.
>
> As Jesus went on from there, he saw a man named

Matthew sitting at the tax collector's booth. "Follow me," he told him, and Matthew got up and followed him. While Jesus was having dinner at Matthew's house, many tax collectors and "sinners" came and ate with him and his disciples. When the Pharisees saw this, they asked the disciples, "Why does your teacher eat with tax collectors and 'sinners'?" On hearing this, Jesus said, "It is not the healthy who need a doctor, but the sick. But go and learn what this means: '. . . I have not come to call the righteous, but sinners.'" (Matthew 9:1-13)

Jesus was a fundamentalist in his faith.

Jesus healed the paralyzed man by forgiving his sins. In so doing, Jesus ascribed to himself the powers of God. The Jews believed that only God could forgive sin, so if Jesus forgave sin, he made himself equal to God. He did not deny who he was to soften their criticism.

Jesus also said, "Repent, for the kingdom of heaven is near" (Matthew 4:17); "You must be born again" (John 3:7); and "I am the way and the truth and the life. No one comes to the Father except through me" (John 14:6-7). Jesus was saying there is only one way to God, and it's a narrow way.

Fundamentalists have a narrow message built upon uncompromising beliefs. When it came to his identity, message, and calling, Jesus was uncompromising. He held firmly to the absolutes of his faith in the Father and never once diluted the Good News, regardless of the circumstances, the audience, or the consequences.

The Pharisees represented the religious establishment of their day, and keeping the law was part of their self-image of holiness, whereas Jesus lived the "new law" of personal relationship with God. Pharisees placed a high value on the form of their faith; Christ placed a higher value on its life-giving vitality. The Pharisees were hypocrites because they pretended to be holy when they were not. Jesus was holy and never denied who he was.

Jesus was evangelical in his lifestyle.

Jesus knew that he was going to the Cross. He preached, taught, ate, drank, healed, and broke boundaries to fulfill his purpose. He was a man of intention, who took the initiative in advancing the kingdom of God at every opportunity and at all costs. Evangelicals are also the bearers and sharers of good news.

God gave us hands and feet so we could work and serve him. It isn't someone else's job to build the kingdom, but yours and mine. Jesus is our model. You and I are hypocrites when we pay more attention to a person's reputation than to a true understanding of their brokenness and need. We are hypocrites if we pay more attention to the shortcomings of others than we do to our own. What does your lifestyle communicate to others? Are you relevant, truthful, and loving? Do you dare to call yourself an evangelical?

Jesus was liberal in his relationships.

A liberal person has a free and widespread association with people who don't know Jesus. Liberals continually affirm the dignity of all people, even if this compromises their reputations. They share Jesus with them without recklessly abandoning the wisdom of biblical teaching.

In his relationships, Jesus was generous, broad-minded, tolerant, and free of the preconceived notions of religious orthodoxy. As a rabbi, Jesus was prohibited by rabbinical teachings from associating with people of immoral reputation, but Jesus went where the need was greatest. He did not come to save self-satisfied people who were convinced that they didn't need help. He came to minister to people who were desperately aware of their need for a Savior.

The Pharisees were more concerned with preserving their ceremonial purity than with helping another sinful person. They offered criticism, not encouragement, and practiced a religion of condemnation rather than forgiveness. They modeled outward orthodoxy in place of inward transformation and practical help. Christ did not call us to the safety of the Pharisee; he called us to the risk of the Cross. For each of these reasons, the words *fundamentalist, evangelical,* and *liberal* should apply to our lives in God.

Nineteen years ago, I founded the work of The Gathering in Columbus, Ohio. From day one, we determined to model these three values. As a result, I've taken some hits along the way from a number of well-meaning religious people.

One time, I was challenged by a friend for associating with a local businessman. My friend said, "I know this man and he's unethical. I don't approve of him. Why is he involved in The Gathering?"

I responded, "We exist for men and women like him. We're not a closed-door, members-only religious society. On the day that Christ found us, we were no different than he is." My friend never really got it. He was spending too much time labeling, segmenting, and categorizing people to have time to reach out to them.

In February, someone called the office to question my wisdom in having a certain political leader participate in one of our events. He told me everything that was wrong with this person and his political views. I listened and calmly communicated these three values to her, but she totally missed it. To my way of thinking, this leader was going to hear the same message as the last person at the last table in the back of the room.

I'll undergo guilt by association any time, if Jesus is the reason.

When I signed up to follow Jesus, I was not a member of the "Already Perfect" club. If I read Scripture correctly, Jesus mixed it up with others in the real world. He didn't stand on the sidelines and picket. If he were here today and wanted to reach alcoholic bikers, he wouldn't protest outside the local bar. He would go inside, sit down, and talk to someone. He wouldn't be offended by the smell of cigarette smoke on his clothes, and he would probably be wearing blue jeans and not a robe.

How do you get the "beer drinking bikers" out of the bars without first going into the bars to befriend them? How do you host a funeral service with one thousand people in black leather and studs for a biker killed in a traffic accident unless you already have a relevant and authentic relationship based on the person of Jesus? How do you get hundreds to show up each year for the "biker blessing" service unless there is an intentional, persistent plan of action motivated by love? The men of Grove City Church of the Nazarene have such a relationship, and this is a testimony to their fundamentalist-evangelical-liberal passion.

What values guide your life's vision, passion, and purpose? How do they help you reach your desired outcomes? Are you pursuing them without compromise? How will your world be different one year from today because of your commitment to your core values?

REFLECTIONS

What are the top three core values of your life?

How is it possible to be a fundamentalist, an evangelical, and a liberal at the same time?

What have you learned from Jesus that will change how you live your life from now on?

ACTIONS

Find a way to relate to, connect with, and show love to one person whom you have previously alienated, judged, or criticized.

Write down your answers to the following questions:

Why do you believe that having a relationship with God is more powerful, effective, and righteous than relying upon religious convention?

What is one thing you will do to show love and dignity to people who are treated as outcasts by your peer group?

NO MORE NEW YEAR'S RESOLUTIONS!

USING GOALS TO ACHIEVE YOUR LIFE'S MISSION

Taking life seriously glorifies God; taking life flippantly glorifies man.

Setting goals for life, with purpose and commitment, guarantees progress to all.

—PETER DANIELS

THEY WERE PERENNIAL "also-rans" to the most successful professional sports franchise in history, the mighty pin-striped New York Yankees. Unlike the storied teams of Ruth, Gehrig, Mantle, Maris, and DiMaggio, this hapless ball club suffered for eighty-six years with a legacy of futility matched by only one other team in major league baseball history. They were known by their battle cries of "Reverse the Curse," and "Wait 'til next year!"

They were the Boston Red Sox.

They had almost magically squandered every opportunity to win the World Series during my lifetime and the lifetimes of octogenarians from Boston to Bar Harbor. They had been beaten by singles hitters driving home runs over the Green Monster in left field, and they were beaten again by slowly bounding balls that rolled between the legs of first basemen.

Even I succumbed to the curse.

I left Fenway Park—the home of my beloved BoSox—in the summer of 1998 at the end of the eighth inning of the only game I have ever watched them play in person. "We" had just lost the lead and were down two runs, so I picked myself up and left the ball park to beat the crowd. I arrived at my hotel only to learn that Mo Vaughn had delivered my team from defeat with a dramatic game-ending, game-winning, three-run home run in the bottom of the ninth inning. I had lost the faith, and in so doing, I missed my only opportunity ever to be with them when they won a game, let alone in such dramatic fashion.

The 2004 season was just another year of porous defense and underachieving pitching, with the Red Sox once again finishing as runners-up to the elite New York Yankees. The Red Sox hadn't won a World Series since 1918, when Babe Ruth was in their pitching rotation. There was no reason to believe that this year would be any different, but that was before a group of self-proclaimed idiots—a supposed Jesus Christ look-alike (Johnny Damon); Big Papi (David Ortiz), the ever-smiling, larger-than-life baseball player from the Dominican Republic; an aging, injured pitcher (Curt Schilling)—an enterprising physician (Dr. Bill Morgan), and a cadaver (identity unknown) conspired to destroy the status quo and win the World Series.

In the first round of the American League playoffs, Boston swept the Anaheim Angels three games to none, with David Ortiz hitting the game-winning, playoff-clinching home run in the bottom of the tenth inning of Game 3. Next up were those fearsome New York Yankees, who quickly took an insurmountable three games to none lead.

> No major-league team had ever rallied from a 3-0 deficit to even a seven-game series, let alone win it. But the Red Sox, self-proclaimed "idiots," insisted they were too stupid to be intimidated by their predicament. Things got more dire when the Yankees took a 4-3 lead into the ninth inning of Game 4, with star closer Mariano Rivera on the mound.[1]

The end was just moments away; one more win for the Yankees, and they would return to the World Series; three more outs for the Red Sox, and it was "wait 'til next year!" Somehow, from deep within, the Red Sox managed to tie the score against the most dominant relief pitcher in baseball. Then, in the twelfth inning, they rose to victory on a home run by David Ortiz. Less than twenty-four hours later, Ortiz delivered again, with a game-winning single in the bottom of the fourteenth inning.

With this win came the stark reality that they must leave the friendly confines of Fenway Park, return to Yankee Stadium down three games to two, and put a "stitched together," thirty-eight-year-old pitcher on the mound against the New York Yankees in "the House that Ruth Built." Curt Schilling went to the mound with a severely displaced ankle tendon that had been sewn into place by Dr. Bill Morgan ("to keep it from flopping around"), only after he had practiced this radical and unprecedented procedure on a cadaver.

> The blood, a bright crimson upon pure white, seeped into the sanitary sock of Red Sox pitcher Curt Schilling around his ankle, like stigmata for true believers in the fanatical church of Boston baseball. His wounds were real, as real as those of New England baseball fans over the past 86 unfulfilled years; Schilling's ankle was so badly mangled that he would have been undergoing surgery and a three-month rehabilitation if not for the little matter of pitching Game 2 of the World Series.[2]

Every pitch was an effort for Schilling; it required total dedication and total focus, and brought pain and pressure to the tendon, the ankle, and the sutures. With blood seeping through his sock from the sutures, Schilling beat the Yankees and forced Game 7.

In reality, Game 6 completed the ultimate comeback. The sight of a "one-legged" pitcher throwing with such command seemed to be the ultimate defeat of the Yankees. They returned for Game 7, but never seemed to show up.

The goal of going to the World Series was quickly realized in Game 7. Derek Lowe pitched one-hit ball for six innings as he shut down the powerful Yankee lineup. David Ortiz homered again, Johnny Damon hit a grand slam, and with a final score of 10-3, the Red Sox were going to the World Series!

Four games and four wins over the National League champion St. Louis Cardinals, and one more winning "sutured blood and guts" performance by Schilling, and the Red Sox had their coveted trophy and their first World Series championship in eighty-six years!

Schilling's bloody, gutsy performance, Ortiz's dramatic clutch hitting, and Damon's long hair and beard drove the sports world to follow this story daily, but another factor had made the impossible possible.

Eleven months earlier, the Red Sox had traded with the Arizona Diamondbacks to obtain the rights to Schilling. They hoped that his addition to the pitching staff would be the final piece of the puzzle needed to take the franchise where it had not been in eight decades.

They were right. The goal was to win the World Series, and the ownership took every step possible to supply the team with the winning talent. The manager led and motivated his men, and the players established a clubhouse closeness that carried over to inspired execution on the baseball diamond. Their goal was accomplished.

Throughout the course of the American League Championship Series and the World Series, the TV cameras repeatedly focused on Schilling's ankle and on his demeanor as he sat in the dugout between innings with a towel draped around his shoulders. On occasion, Schilling would pick up a dog-eared spiral notebook and study it carefully.

He did this often. He was studying his game plan and doing everything he could to prepare himself mentally for the next inning. Curt Schilling keeps a detailed log of every at bat of every opposing hitter he has pitched against. After every game, he makes notes on any changes. This allows him to write a specific game plan for each batter he faces in every game. When preparing for players he has never pitched against, he watches tapes of other pitchers who have pitched against the batters he is to face.

Schilling's first goal is to be in the best physical shape possible. Goal two is to prepare mentally for every batter he will face. Goal

three is to give his best in the clubhouse and on the baseball diamond. Goal four is to put his team in the best position possible
to win every game he pitches. Goal five is to always give his best
to his team so that they can win the World Series. Goal six is to
glorify God's name. Objective reached, goals accomplished!

Curt Schilling knew his mission and set specific goals to help
him pursue and achieve it. His joy came in competing, which he
did well because he had prepared well. He prepared well because
he set goals that pushed him to succeed and to be his very best.
His best resulted in the World Series ring.

Our best will result in something different, but we cannot do
our best without goals. I believe that life is more than time spent,
and that goals deepen, fulfill, and extend life. God has given us
a limited time frame to use wisely in pursuit of a purpose that
benefits others and the world we will leave behind.

I have come to believe that God uses people, their personal
mission, and their goals to change the world. However, many of
us are not very good at pursuing our personal mission through
life goals. As a result, we sell ourselves short and limit what God
does through us.

I think that we often equate goal-setting with making New
Year's resolutions. Too often, they are driven by shortness of
breath and expanding waistlines. We are pushed toward them
by failure rather than drawn to them by the passion within us.
When you tie your goals to your mission, you are already halfway
toward their completion.

For most people, goal setting is intimidating and complicated,
but when we take an honest look at them, goals can actually
be the pathway to freedom and success. Goal setting is simply

determining today what you will pursue tomorrow. It's a matter of making up our minds in advance as to how we will realize our mission. It's figuring out where we want to go and how we will get there.

In his book *Holy Sweat*, Tim Hansel states, "If you don't boldly choose your own goals, you are destined to accept someone else's goals. But very few of us take the time to write down specific goals for where we want to end up. Hazy goals inevitably produce hazy results. We need to write down clearly defined, vividly imagined goals that are packed with emotion."[3]

It is the emotion of our goals that gives them power in our lives. Passion married to mission is an unstoppable force. Are your goals in writing? A goal that isn't written down is only wishful thinking.

When you write your goals, you empower yourself. The golfer who practices the putt in his mind and the baseball player who sees the ball coming off his bat and falling into left field for a hit are more successful than those who don't rehearse their game plan. As you write the goal, you see it, and as you see it, you see it fulfilled.

Several years ago, I was relegated to running indoors during the winter on a small track that required twenty-six laps to complete a mile. How boring! Believe it or not, I survived for the required length of time by envisioning the apostle Paul running fifteen yards in front of me on short, stumpy, determined legs! If he could do it, I could do it. And I did it! I carry my goals with me daily and ignore them (within reason) on the weekends, which is one of my goals.

Would you do me a favor? Would you get a blank piece of paper right now? Don't skip this part—it isn't just a silly exercise. It might make a huge difference in your life.

At the top of this "life chart," write your personal mission. It might be a word, a phrase, or a short paragraph. You may need to review chapter 7 to reach clarity about this. Under your life mission, create five columns with the following headings:

Relationship with God: This is about your spiritual journey, your walk with Jesus, prayer, meditation, silence, worship, Bible study, and Scripture memory. How will you spend time with God? What will that relationship look like a year from now?

Personal Growth: These are things such as education, recreation, reading, physical health, hobbies, creative expression, emotional health, social relationships, friendships, rest, retreat, renewal, and dreams. How will you grow as a person?

Family: These things concern your relationship with your spouse and his or her nurture, affirmation, and cultivation; your children and their discipline, health, education, athletics, social life, and spiritual well-being; immediate and extended family; holidays and vacations; and finances. How will you benefit your family?

Career: These matters pertain to your vocation and each of the areas required for your growth, success, and advancement. How will your work reflect God? If it's just a job, find something else to do!

Community and World: This area includes your church, community, and missions involvement, and how you relate to worthy organizations and causes in your neigh-

borhood and the world. How will the world benefit from
your presence?

Spend some time thinking about each of these categories and
whatever specific goals under each category will help you to
achieve your personal mission. Some categories might have only
one goal, while others might have more.

Some of your goals will reflect what you are obligated to do,
regardless of desire. Others will reflect interests that you desire
deeply, and some will flow from your commitments and love for
God and others.

You may need to work on this for a while. Write down your
goals, and scratch some out when it becomes clear that they don't
serve your personal mission in life. Write down new ones as you
creatively "think outside the box." One of my unusual goals is
to experience God's grace through nature every day of my life. I
hear more birds, see more animals, and experience the beauty of
God's creation more than anyone I know. When is the last time
you marveled at the fog rising off the ground, driven to the sky
by the warming rays of sunlight breaking through the morning
clouds?

Once you feel comfortable with the goals you've established,
assign a time frame to each goal. Think in terms of short-, mid-,
and long-term time frames. My short-term goals are thirty to
ninety days, mid-term goals are four to twelve months, and long-
term goals extend to three, five, and ten years. I'm just beginning
on goals that will take me to age eighty.

Once your goals are clear and time frames have been assigned,
think through each goal to determine the action steps needed to
achieve them. Those steps may change from time to time, and
they may need to be updated each year. They will become your
guide and your friend, keeping you on track as they align with

your mission. If you begin to struggle, consider whether the goal is still appropriate or if God is moving you in a new direction. These steps are your strategy for achieving your goals.

You might want to write this life plan in a story form, with each goal and action step told in sentences and paragraphs. The key is to write them down and begin to picture their completion in your mind. You might prefer to put this in outline form or make a chart. The outline of your life chart could look something like this:

PERSONAL MISSION

Relationship with God

Goal 1:	Goal 2:
Step 1:	*Step 1:*
Step 2:	*Step 2:*
Step 3:	*Step 3:*

Personal Growth

Goal 1:	Goal 2:
Step 1:	*Step 1:*
Step 2:	*Step 2:*
Step 3:	*Step 3:*

Family

Goal 1:	Goal 2:
Step 1:	*Step 1:*
Step 2:	*Step 2:*
Step 3:	*Step 3:*

Career

Goal 1:	Goal 2:
Step 1:	*Step 1:*
Step 2:	*Step 2:*
Step 3:	*Step 3:*

Community and World

Goal 1:	Goal 2:
Step 1:	*Step 1:*
Step 2:	*Step 2:*
Step 3:	*Step 3:*

The form you use should suit your personal preferences as long as it helps you to think through what you want your life to be and how to get there. To some people, this sounds like a lot of work, but when you think of it as an investment in your life, your future, and your mission on earth, it's not that big of a commitment.

Peter Daniels is a highly successful Australian entrepreneur. In one of his books, he writes, "Just as there are laws relating to physics, there are ground rules for goal-setters. You break those rules at your peril. Keep those laws and you will succeed. The world will keep going without you, but you cannot keep going without involvement in the world."[4]

Daniels identifies five guidelines for goal setting:

1. *Clearly define your life goals in terms of ultimate achievement.*
   This allows you to trade your unknown future for a known future. It identifies your direction and desire and places you in a position of accountability that will guide you to new heights of personal success and greater contribution to the

well-being of others. Each large goal must be augmented by intermediate and short-term objectives that logically and effectively lead to success.

2. *Set out your strategy.* Strategy refers to those steps you wrote for achieving each goal. Daniels suggests measuring those steps in terms of time, quality, and quantity. Daniels has set the attainment of his life goals at eighty years of age. At what age will you reach yours? Is your dream big enough and bold enough for eighty years, or will you settle for retirement? Plan the details of what you will need, and erect milestones to gauge your progress.

3. *Plan out the problem areas in advance.* Most people hit an emotional wall of pain, disappointment, fear and self-doubt at some point because they don't adequately prepare for the obstacles that will arise. Are you prepared physically, emotionally, and spiritually for the road ahead? Someone once said, "Worry is an old woman with a bowed head carrying a sack of feathers that she thinks is lead." What will hold you accountable to your objective? What financial and human resource capital is required? Do you have it? How will you get it? Are you logistically advantaged? Have you laid a foundation that wil! launch you with confidence?

4. *Build in reserves.* The world is spinning faster toward a 24/7/365 pace of human existence, but the people who sustain success over extended periods of time value rest, renewal, and refreshment. I start early, but I also retire early. At some time in every day, week, and year, you must walk away from the pursuit of immediate goals to refresh and

replenish yourself. To do this, you will need the love and support of people around you who are committed to you.

5. *Everything you stress inwardly or on paper needs to be examined within a limited time frame.* There is no need to rush to accomplish all of the goals at the same pace, with the same force, at the same time. God gives us life patterns and intends for us to overlap and arrange goals so that they do not compete with one another. Give yourself the freedom to wait five years for this and ten years for that. Your goals must be mutually supportive, not competitive. When you are stymied, recalibrate the time frames. You will arrive sooner at some goals and later at others, but you must establish limited time frames within which to operate.[5]

The next chapter will bring all five of these principles into focus.

REFLECTIONS

How do your goals reflect your mission in life?

How do your goals reflect your heartfelt passions?

Why will you succeed with your goals now, whereas in the past you failed at them?

JOINING UP

SETTING GOALS OF POWER, PASSION, AND PRINCIPLE

*Goals that are connected to our inner life have the
power of passion and principle. They're fueled by
the fire within and based on "true north" principles
that create quality-of-life results.*

—STEPHEN COVEY

MONTY ROBERTS IS known as the real "Horse Whisperer." During
his remarkable lifetime, he has developed a method of "starting"
(taming) wild horses called "join-up" that allows him to communicate with the mustangs as he puts a halter, bridle, saddle, and
rider on their backs within the brief span of thirty minutes.[1]

Monty is author of *The Man Who Listens to Horses,* and he and
his wife, Pat, own and operate Flag Is Up Farms in California.
He has trained horses for the queen of England and has traveled

the world to inform people about his God-given insights into horses and people.

In 1997, Monty Roberts found himself squarely in the cross-hairs of controversy. For decades, his unparalleled success with mustangs and purebreds had been called into question. He did the impossible and was therefore regarded by many as a fraud. The popular belief was that "You can't put a rider on a free-range, just-captured, never-been-touched mustang in thirty minutes," even though Monty did it again and again. He was always under the scrutiny of those who believed that it was somehow a hoax.

In an effort to set the controversy to rest once and for all, Monty accepted a seemingly insurmountable challenge. He agreed to allow a documentary film crew from the BBC and PBS to record his efforts to "join up" in open country with a wild mustang he had dubbed "Shy Boy." Before this attempt, Monty had always accomplished his goals while working with horses in the controlled environment of a round corral—if you can call a situation that pairs an unarmed man with a wild mustang "controlled."

Monty claimed that he had developed a horse language: "I gave this language a name, Equus, and learned how to use it. I found that I could communicate with horses, however wild they were. . . . By using this language, I could have a wild horse following me around as if I were the matriarch."[2] For example, he discovered that an adolescent horse that was out of favor with the dominant mare and sought her acceptance would lick and chew. This is the classic mouthing action of a dependent horse asking for food from a superior. He would also drop his nose to the ground in submission. The matriarch would turn, show her flank, and avoid eye contact. These were signs that the offender had been forgiven and could reenter the herd.

This language was the key to his success.

He wondered what would happen if he were to take his horse, rope, his equestrian language of "join-up," and the five fused vertebrae of his injured back into the uncontrolled environment of the open range.

Could the process work without the round corral? Could it be done at all? Would the scrutiny of the cameras and crew of the BBC and PBS interfere? As a boy, he had gentled wild horses alone on the open landscape. Could he do it again?

The English word *mustang* is derived from the Spanish *mestengo,* for "stray beast." Mustangs are most naturally themselves in the wild. Getting close to Shy Boy would be the first hurdle. Because mustangs are under the authority of the Bureau of Land Management, Monty had to "adopt" several wild horses, including Shy Boy, transport them to his farm, and quickly release them in the high desert of the Cuyama Valley to mix with other free-ranging horses on a privately owned ranch of thousands of acres.

The ride took place on Easter weekend in March 1997. Monty would have to ride for two solid days through the extreme temperatures of the high desert. Could he do that and still achieve "join-up" in the wild?

Monty traveled with three of his horses, an assistant, a five-man wrangler crew carrying supplies, and the ever-present cameras. He wore five layers of clothes for warmth and comfort in fighting the elements. He took pain-killing medication and strapped on his back brace. He would have to locate the herd, find his three mustangs, cut Shy Boy from the herd, and engage the ride.

There was no corral, just Monty on horseback, the mustang, and plenty of room to run. Shy Boy was as wild as a deer. Cut from the herd, he was determined to rejoin it, but Monty continually pressed him from behind and drove him away. They rode throughout the day and into the night, with Shy Boy in flight and glancing back at his unrelenting tracker. Along the way, there were stops for food and water, and finally, the chance for Monty to turn slowly back toward the base camp for a fresh horse and a much-needed warm meal.

Three days later, after nearly one hundred miles of riding, the impossible happened. Sensing that flight would not release him from his human tracker, Shy Boy began to display ear, head, and body movements suggesting that he might want to "join-up" with Monty. Over a period of hours, he stopped, turned his head, began to lick and chew, lowered his ears, dropped his head, and "asked" to join up. He looked at Monty and allowed Monty to touch him. When he was spooked, he ran. Monty let him go, and he returned.

Trust and cooperation were beginning to build. It was time to sleep, after thirty-six exhausting hours in the saddle.

On day three, man and horse stood, walked, and talked together. Slowly, there was progress from touch of hand to rope, blanket, bridle, and saddle. Finally, Shy Boy accepted a foot in the stirrup, a leg over his back, and a rider in the saddle. Within five minutes, he was a relaxed horse. The impossible had happened.

Two years later, Monty faced another set of questions, and he set out to answer them.

If Shy Boy could return to the wild, would he go?

Was he better off wild or domesticated?

What would he choose if given the choice?

Shy Boy would decide.

With the camera crew on hand, Shy Boy was taken on a cattle drive and left near his original free-range herd. Released from his halter, he raced off to rejoin the herd, disappearing into the dimming twilight. At 6:00 A.M., there was still no sign of him. After breakfast, the details of the cattle drive were wrapped up and preparations were made for leaving.

I looked up sharply and I could see movement in the sage. There was a single horse, about three hundred yards to the north, on a hill above us. The rising sun cast a bright light across the ridge, and we could see clearly that he was moving in our direction. The horse trotted right to the center of a clearing in the sagebrush and stopped, like an actor pausing on a stage. . . .

Everybody in the camp was stunned into silence. Shy Boy remained motionless. . . . [Then], with a deliberate movement, [he] turned his head to look back in the direction of the herd. He held that position for a few seconds, then looked toward the camp. He lowered his head and began to walk. . . .

As he reached the edge of the clearing, his head lifted and he broke into a trot, coming squarely in our direction now. . . .

Some two hundred and fifty yards from the camp, he broke into a full gallop. There seemed to be a path through the sage and he followed it in zigzag fashion. . . .

Running at a full gallop straight toward us, Shy Boy gave a loud, clear whinny.

We did not move a muscle. I wore a big smile and stood happily in his path. He galloped full out and only at the last second did he apply the brakes and come to a halt a few yards in front of me so I could step forward and welcome him in. Shy Boy had chosen to come home.[3]

Monty Roberts and his crew perfectly executed the goal-setting guidelines we discussed earlier. There was a clearly defined goal and a determined strategy that took problems into account in advance (food, fresh horses, medical supplies, layered clothing).

They used reserves (a crew of five) within a limited (three-day) time frame.

In spite of the physical suffering Monty endured in this mini-endurance saga of man and horse, he loved every minute of it! This painful and difficult experience brought joy because it was tied to Monty's passion and mission and was made possible by his commitment to his goals.[4]

Goals allow us to experience the depth and fullness of our humanity and of God's grace. If there had been no goals, there would have been no Shy Boy, no memories, and no story to tell. God has stories for you to tell. Do you know what they might be? Your goals may open the doorway to a lifetime of storytelling that will keep you busy and fulfilled until you are eighty or more.

As I have become a goal-setter, I have become more appreciative of this practice. Goals apply the pressure that motivates me to be my best. When combined with the passion of call, purpose, and mission, they propel me forward with a freedom that most people do not experience. They give me the satisfaction and confidence of knowing where I am going.

I have found it necessary to internalize what I've written on paper so that my goals become a part of me that I carry wherever I go. I frequently review my goals and my progress. Some goals change as new information becomes available or as resources or circumstances change. You will need to be aware of your environment and the feedback you receive along the way. The input of friends who are free to communicate with you about blind spots in your life will be invaluable.

Make yourself accountable to someone. Will it be your wife, husband, corporate coach, pastor, friend, or small group? Find a mentor who has been where you are going, or who is committed to your well-being and to the direction you are taking. A good mentor will take satisfaction in your success. Such a person will nurture, challenge, and care for you and be sold on helping you achieve even your wildest dreams.

Some days, I seem to plod towards my goals, and on other days I am caught up on eagle's wings. You need a mentor on both kinds of days. Your mentor must love you—and have the authority to kick you in the seat of the pants! You need someone to keep you in touch with reality while participating in your dreams and encouraging you to fly higher.

While Monty Roberts was taming a wild mustang on the open range, in 1977, I was trying to "join up" with an alienated, angry, and bitter seventeen-year-old boy. It was new territory for me—I didn't have Monty's history of success. I was a willing tenderfoot with a mentor, Rich Van Pelt, who counseled, guided, and encouraged me.

From 1977 to 1981, I was a chaplain for youth offenders at Denver Juvenile Hall. Matt was one of the very first kids I met. He was in custody for the rape and sexual assault of seventeen women, mostly nurses who worked at a downtown hospital. Matt eyed me up and down without saying much and moved to a corner table to play solitaire.

I spent my first day in his unit hanging out with kids, playing cards, and counseling a boy on his way to court. Later, I joined B-Unit on the basketball court. I held my own with Matt and scored enough points to earn a bit of respect in his eyes.

Our connection began with bumping, running, passing, shooting, and intermingling our sweat. The basketball game with others became a one-on-one between the two of us. Basketball was followed by a game of cards, and cards led to conversation.

Conversation led to questions.

"If God made marijuana, then what's wrong with smoking it?"

"If I've been hurt by my dad, what's wrong with my hurting others?"

"Why should I care about anyone else, since no one cares about me?"

"How could anyone, even God, forgive me for what I've done?"

Conversations led to relationship, and then to Matt's guarded disclosure of his story. He gradually began to shadow me on his unit, on the court, and at Bible study. At times, I was deeply disappointed in him for messing up, but I never stopped trying to befriend him. All the while, the message never changed: "If you can't trust God, can you at least trust me? I can offer you friendship, but only God can offer you forgiveness, wholeness, and freedom."

In time, Matt let the walls down and discovered forgiveness from God, which opened a new doorway in his life. This story wasn't played out on a world stage with camera and crew. It took place in a dingy, dirty juvenile jail, seen by no one. Three things were key: my mission, my goals, and my strategy.

My mission of serving as God's instrument in revealing his love to a lost world helped me to see the need in Matt's life and to begin caring for him. I created goals to enter his world, meet him at his point of need, persistently offer him hope, and stay until the mission of redemption and restoration was accomplished. Under Rich's mentorship, I developed a strategy to build a relationship based upon common interests that would allow Matt to open his life up to me first and then to the God he was so angry with.

Goals are the stirrups that steady a rider when the horse is running at full gallop. They make the ride better and safer. Goals, strategy, and mission go hand in hand. There would be no book in your hands if every Tuesday evening and every Friday of the past three years, I hadn't set aside time to write. I also phoned, faxed, and e-mailed friends, acquaintances, strangers, agents, and publishers for nearly two years before someone accepted my manuscript.

I could easily have succumbed to doubts and discouragement from the multitude of rejections I received, but I was on a mission, I had a big goal, and I had a strategy. I held each of these close to my heart, and I never gave up.

What have you yet to do that is now undone?

Why not do it?

Why not begin now?

If not now, when?

ACTIONS

Write down three specific goals for your life that support your mission.

Write down a specific time frame for each of your goals and indicate how you are going to measure progress.

Share your goals with a trusted friend or mentor and ask him or her to hold you accountable.

WRITE YOUR NAME ON THE UNIVERSE!

LEAVING A LEGACY

What we do in life echoes in eternity.

—FROM THE MOVIE *Gladiator*

WHAT IS YOUR LEGACY? What of yourself will live on in the lives of others after you are gone? What will you pass along to your successors? It's your choice. No one else, even the author of your obituary, can make this decision. It's determined by what you did yesterday and what you do today.

Occasionally, it's worth taking a humorous look at a serious topic.

As the story goes, a pastor, a priest, and a rabbi attended a funeral to pay their respects to a fellow clergyman. A friend approached and asked, "When you are in your casket and friends and family gather around to mourn your death, what would you like them to say about you?"

The pastor responded, "I'd like them to say that I was a wonderful husband, a fine spiritual leader, and a great family man."

The priest replied, "I would love it if they said that I was an excellent teacher, a servant of God, and someone who made a difference in people's lives."

After a short pause, the rabbi said, "I'd like to hear them say . . . 'Look, he's moving!'"

If we're honest, we would all prefer the rabbi's response over the others. We would all like to hang around in good health for a very, very long time, well beyond the seventy to eighty years granted to us by God. We have unfinished business, and we fear the unknown passage from life to death to new life with God. Only a few of the older, the wiser, and the worn-out are truly ready to go at any time. As children of God, we are moving on to eternity where we will live with him, and we will live on in the hearts of those we leave behind. From that perspective, "Look, he's moving" certainly applies!

Difference makers such as you and I continue to live on in the lives of others. We take redemptive action by connecting with people in a way that creates a reconciling relationship that helps to restore them to God. You have already done things in your life that have influenced others, and today you will add to your legacy through your words, acts, and attitudes. Will you offer hope to those you meet, or will you confirm the despair that so many people feel?

Sometimes we need to take a serious look at a serious topic.

Trent Reznor is the creative writer of the rock group Nine Inch Nails. They are known for such album titles as *Pretty Hate Machine, Broken Halo,* and *The Downward Spiral,* and songs such as "Hurt," "The Day the World Went Away" and "The Art of

Self Destruction." The prevailing philosophy of their music is one of hurt, loss, and grief. Reznor sings of a world where pain is "the only thing that's real." He sings of a world where he is continually disappointed, and where he continually disappoints, and where his only two friends are *escape* and *despair*. He sings of a world where the ultimate hope is to go back to the dirt from whence he came.

You will encounter someone today who needs you, someone in search of hope, truth, answers, or just another human to quietly listen to them or care for them. They will not bear the image of Jesus, but that of hurt. Their bible will be the playlist of Nine Inch Nails, not the Bible of Genesis, Psalms, John, and Revelation. This person needs for you to make a difference in his or her life. You can create a new tomorrow for someone today, and that's a legacy worth leaving.

Here are a few of those "new tomorrows" from my life.

"Hey man, I need to be saved."

That was my introduction to Mark. If ever a chaplain heard seven better words than these during his first day on the job, I cannot imagine what they would be. It was October 1977, and I was about to encounter 120 juvenile offenders at Gilliam Youth Center, also known as the Denver juvenile hall. "Juvy" is located in the heart of inner-city Denver, not far from the strip clubs, prostitutes, crack houses, and drug dealers of Colfax Avenue. At the time, four thousand kids a year were incarcerated in Juvenile Hall, with an average stay of two and a half days.

It was a high-risk, fast-paced human turnstile.

It was my job to provide Bible studies, worship, counseling, volunteers, recreation, and social events for these young people.

What can one person do with four thousand kids slipping through his fingers like sand?

"She's like every other prostitute who comes through these doors."

It was a cold, hard slap of reality. Tammy was back in lockup. For her, it was a revolving-door history of poverty, instability, emotional abuse by her mother, and sexual abuse from her mother's boyfriends. This resulted in drug addiction that she paid for with prostitution. Where else could she go? In her world, the only option was the street.

What began on the street always ended in the back of a police car and the return trip to jail. She was slight of build and had bare patches of scalp showing through her short hair. Somehow, she managed a sad but beautiful smile and a soft demeanor despite her anxiety. What could a twenty-six-year-old white male do for a sixteen-year-old black girl whose life was defiled by men?

Infant Sexually Assaulted by Teen

If ever I felt the urge to do serious physical damage to someone, it came while reading this headline in the *Rocky Mountain News.*

What would possess anyone to molest an eighteen-month-old baby girl?

I wanted revenge, and in a few short hours I would be facing the accused. What was I to do? What could I offer to someone so morally depraved and perverted that he would sexually assault a baby?

∾

"Mr. Hook, you'd better bring the girl in now; her father wants you arrested for kidnapping and rape."

What do you do when you receive a phone call from a friend who is providing refuge for a fourteen-year-old girl seeking protection from her physically abusive father? I met with my friend and her teenage runaway Shelly to listen and formulate a plan for reconciliation with her father.

I couldn't just take her back home, and I didn't yet know all the facts. I phoned Shelly's dad, and he wanted his daughter back, period. He had no interest in counseling, mediation, or social services. It was just, "Bring her back now!"

But what if Shelly was telling the truth? What if I was returning her to a hostile, abusive home? I phoned the Jefferson County Sheriff's Department to present our dilemma and seek their intervention. That's when I was informed of her father's request for my arrest. What was her fate? What would mine be?

This is but a small part of the story I have written with my life. It's part of my legacy. It's a history passed on to me by others, and then passed from me to others who follow me at the juvenile hall. I was simply the next person in line.

"Hey man, I need to be saved."

Mark, the young man who said these words to me, prayed with me that Tuesday afternoon and asked God to forgive his sins. He took responsibility for his actions, accepted counsel, participated in a small group, and soon left my life, never to return. I touched him for three weeks, and then he was gone.

"She's like every *other* prostitute."

Tammy never was "like every other prostitute that came through those doors." She was a unique person of worth who was caught in a terrible trap. She met me and then she met Jesus. We slowly built a close, caring relationship and established trust. One day, she drew a picture and asked me to look at it. She said, "I was thinking of you and when I did, I saw Jesus. So I drew this picture of him."

I introduced her to men who behaved as God intended. She returned on two more occasions, and eventually corresponded and sent a photo from a home where her life was being pieced together.

"Infant sexually assaulted by teen."

Hector and I were never close. I don't know if it was the shame of his sexual assault or the brokenness of his pain-filled life. We met, we talked, and I continually sought to befriend him. Our relationship was always a stretch, always a reach, and never a connection.

I felt that he was going through the motions. I don't know where he is today, but I never gave him any less than I gave to any other kid. Maybe the next person carrying the legacy of Jesus in their life was able to reach him.

"Mr. Hook, bring the girl in now."

Seven years later, on a return visit to Denver, I spoke at my former church. Unknown to me, Shelly was in the service. She approached me with a huge smile and reintroduced herself as "the runaway girl." She thanked me for risking so much to assist her.

This help and attention spurred Shelly to further investigate a relationship with God. She, her dad, and her family had reunited, and she was pursing her faith and her career. She was married and expecting her first child. She had a new life that she could not even imagine when she was on the run from her dad. I played a part in her new life.

These are everyday stories of the lives of everyday people.

At the time they happened, I had no thought of leaving a legacy or of how big a difference I was making. I simply wanted to do the right thing to help another person. We don't always know when we will make a difference.

REFLECTIONS

How has your life already changed the course of history?

What will you now do with your life to change the world forever?

What of your life will live on in the lives of others after you are gone?

LIVING IN THE LION'S DEN

PERSISTENCE AND DOUBT

You gotta serve somebody. It may be the
devil, or it may be the Lord, but
you gotta serve somebody.

—BOB DYLAN

WHEN WE THINK of legacy leavers and difference makers, we often think of people such as Alexander the Great, Joan of Arc, Winston Churchill, John F. Kennedy, Martin Luther King, Jr., and Mother Teresa. A close examination of their lives reveals that they were just ordinary people exercising the disciplines of influence on a micro level. They had a destiny for influence before God dropped them into a bigger pond for macro impact. Very likely, if we had approached them during their lifetimes and told them that they were having a cultural impact, they would have said, "I'm just doing my job."

In his book *Living in the Lions' Den without Being Eaten,* William Carr Peel defines influence as "the power or capacity to produce desired results, to impact or to cause some change to take place."[1] Influence changes people from the inside out. Influence changes thoughts, thoughts change behavior, and behavior changes cultures. Peel has a formula: Competence + Character + Courage = Great Influence. When you are doing the right thing at the right time for the right reasons, you are exerting a powerful influence.

As an individual, you can make all the difference. There is extraordinary power in an ordinary life. Here is another ordinary person. You may not have heard of him, but he influenced the course of history and made it possible for Abraham Lincoln, Dr. Martin Luther King, Jr., and many others to follow in his steps. He was a short man who has cast an eternal shadow.

William Wilberforce was five feet tall. He lived in a world of "haves" and "have-nots." Low-lying clouds and fog covered London, reflecting the shadowy hearts and minds of many rich, politically powerful, and spiritually dead people who inhabited that dark city in 1787.

Families were torn apart as children were forced to work in the mines and mills of the countryside, and slave ships plied the oceans, carrying human cargo to the West Indian plantations to serve the appetites of the wealthy and privileged. Wilberforce was not quite thirty years old, but he was already a political veteran who had won the Yorkshire seat in the British House of

Commons. He grew increasingly disturbed by the decadent life-styles that were financed on the backs of slaves.

Early one Sunday morning in 1787, he poured out his heart in his journal. "Almighty God has set before me two great objectives—the abolition of the slave trade and the reformation of morals."

William Wilberforce was a David among Goliaths. He slowly recruited support, and within a year, he was able to successfully spearhead the passage of a bill that limited the number of slaves to be transported on each ship. It was not a major victory, but it was a small, persistent step in the right direction.

In 1791, the opposition rebuffed any new laws and pressed in with a chorus of voices that, translated into today's world of sound bites, would be, "It's the economy, stupid! Show me the money!" They believed that the abolition of slavery would be the downfall of the British economy.

In 1792, Wilberforce mobilized many of the commoners to boycott West Indian sugar, but even this failed to bring new legislation. Time after time, he and his abolitionist friends were defeated, but still they pressed on. Belief in the dignity of all mankind and the fellowship of Jesus sustained him during those years. The friendship of a few men and women of faith and character lifted his head and moved his heart. One such brother sent him this note:

> Unless God has raised you up for this very thing, you will be worn out by the opposition of men and devils, but if God be for you, who can be against you? Are all of them together stronger than God? Oh, be not weary in well doing. Go on in the name of God, and in the power of his might, till even American slavery, the vilest that ever saw the sun, shall vanish away before it. That he

that has guided you from your youth up may continue to strengthen in this and all things.

Your affectionate servant,

John Wesley.[2]

Finally, after twenty years, the bill to abolish the slave trade was passed on February 4, 1807. Wilberforce was elated with this stunning victory for all slaves under English rule, but he had one hill left to climb—he wanted total freedom for all existing slaves. Three days before his death and forty-six years into the battle to abolish the slave trade, Parliament passed the Bill for the Abolition of Slavery in 1833.

In many ways, Wilberforce's heart for justice, truth, and the dignity of all people led to the 1863 abolition of slavery in the United States under President Abraham Lincoln. Wilberforce lived for seventy-four years. His determined efforts over many decades led to the abolition of slavery in the British Empire and beyond.

How many thousands of blacks walk free today because of his efforts?

William Wilberforce took redemptive action as he purchased, rescued, and released slaves. He didn't sit and wait, but pursued his cause with passionate opposition to the immoral, accommodating norms of his day. He refused to accept apathy or defeat.

He created reconciling relationships as he worked with others to bring all humans (free and slave) into harmony with God's intended design. He created coalitions and forged alliances that spoke loudly enough to affect the conscience of the masses.

He diligently and faithfully sought to restore all people to God, and he influenced the politicians, leaders, and clergy of his time in such a manner that slaves were returned to their God-ordained place. It was not restored perfectly or immediately, but Wilberforce did the difficult legal work. He showed the way back to God, and he left nothing of his ordinary soul and his extraordinary dreams to be buried in the cemetery.[3]

I love this excerpt from a poem by Dr. Myles Munroe:

> *The wealthiest place on earth is not the gold mines*
> *of the world,*
> *not the diamond mines of the world, not the oil fields*
> *of the world,*
> *not even the platinum mines of the world.*
> *The wealthiest place on earth is the cemetery. . . .*
> *Buried in the cemetery are dreams that died as dreams,*
> *songs that were never sung,*
> *poetry that was never written, . . .*
> *businesses that were never incorporated.*
> *What . . . tragedy lies in the wealth of the cemetery!*[4]

What of yourself will be buried in the cemetery?

What will you refuse to take to your grave?

What have you not yet left behind for others that you now will do?

What do you want to write on the universe?

What of your life will echo through eternity?

In this book, I've returned occasionally to the theme of doubt because it is something that I struggle with. I'm trying to accept it as a reminder that I'm just like everyone else, rather than as a burden to be borne. It reminds me that I need God and other people.

Perhaps doubt helps me in relating to others. If so, then God can use it. He has never used my arrogance, but he seems to get a lot of mileage out of humility, when I let him. Philip Yancey develops this point very well when he writes, "Reading the biographies of great people of faith, I must search to find one whose faith did not grow on a skeleton of doubt, and indeed grow so that the skeleton eventually became hidden."[5]

Great things are left undone in life, and the cemetery remains full of wealth because of doubt. Did William Wilberforce doubt? Of course he did! Then he took that doubt, infused it with faith, and accompanied it with redemptive action.

Doubt identifies need, need requires Christ, Christ delivers on his promises, and doubt retreats and dies. "Put your finger here; see my hands. Reach out your hand and put it into my side. Stop doubting and believe" (John 20:27).

God is overlaying our skeleton of doubt with muscle. He wants to bury that skeleton deep, deep inside of us so that we become his people of faith. Doubt travels with me daily and has repeatedly returned to your side as you have read this book.

Do not despair about your doubting, but embrace it as a continual opportunity to test all that you believe about God, yourself, others, and the world in which you live.

On December 12, 1988, I had a choice between letting doubt give birth to defeat, or giving doubt to God and allowing him to do something supernatural with it. I gave it to God.

I was six months into my work with The Gathering. I had left my comfort zone of counseling inner-city kids and working with broken families and was now in the world of white-collar success. My clients were surgeons, business owners, community leaders, governors, senators, and civic giants. I was not like them, and I did not have the money to compete with their lifestyles. I worked in donated space on the back side of a building in downtown Columbus. I had to take a hard look at myself and then ask God what he had to say on the subject.

> *Thoughts of a Doubting Man*
> *I am nothing*
> *an insignificant man of 36 years*
> *husband of one wife*
> *father of two daughters.*
> *My office overlooks the back of a gray bank building*
> *I share the street with the homeless, the lost, and the*
>   *depraved.*
> *I am a blink in time*
> *an afterthought in the minds of men*
> *each moving through life*
> *toward his own goals, success, and satisfaction.*
> *I have nothing.*
> *The little I do have, I do not own; it belongs to you.*
> *I search for significance*
> *but I am hounded by doubt.*
> *I strive for success*
> *but continually fall short.*
> *Who I am is not who I want to be. . . .*
> *But I do have a dream*
> *that someday I will be complete in you.*
> *I want to be one of your heroes,*
> *a man of strength, dignity, and vision.*
> *I want to do great things for you*

. . . that will last for eternity.
But once again the dilemma:
I doubt and fear
and have so little to offer you.
All that I have I give to you
it's not much,
is it?
In doing so
I realize
my doubting is a doorway to freedom
my significance is found at the cross
my success is found in seeking you.

God answered:

Unless a kernel of wheat falls to the ground and dies,
it remains only a single seed.
But if it dies, it produces many seeds. . . .
The man who hates his life in this world
will keep it for eternal life.

(JOHN 12:24-25)

Blessed are the humble; yours is the kingdom of God
Blessed are those who mourn; you are comforted
Blessed are the lowly: you have inherited the earth
Blessed are the merciful; you have received mercy
Blessed are the pure in heart; you have seen God
Blessed are the peacemakers; you are a child of God
Blessed are the persecuted; yours is the kingdom of heaven
Blessed are those who hunger and thirst for righteousness; you
    are complete.

(MATTHEW 5:3-10, AUTHOR'S PARAPHRASE)

God took my doubt and returned it to me as completeness.

God's legacy became my legacy, and his legacy is your legacy—of comforted mourners, satisfied hunger, and incompleteness made whole. It's a legacy of little becoming much, death becoming life, and darkness becoming light. It's a legacy of finding strength through weakness and having more with less.

You are totally qualified to leave an enduring legacy. Your little will become much, your common, uncommon, and your ordinary, extraordinary. Your image is God's image. "The foolishness of God is wiser than man's wisdom, and the weakness of God is stronger than man's strength" (1 Corinthians 1:25).

ACTIONS

Write the names of three people—living or dead—who have influenced your life more positively than anyone else in history.

What is the legacy that each of these three left on your life?

Write the epitaph you would like to have inscribed on your headstone.

Write what you will do to ensure that your legacy lives on in the lives of others after you are gone.

CLAIMING YOUR AUTHORITY

THE POWER OF YOUR ORDINARY LIFE

We are not inconsequential.

What we do makes a difference.

God says that you make a big difference.

—JOHN ASHCROFT, FORMER U.S. ATTORNEY GENERAL

"MR. HOOK, YOU have my permission to work with one kid. If you succeed, you'll have as many kids to work with as you can handle. If you fail, then you'll never get another kid from me." Such was my introduction to the unsmiling, six-foot-four-inch Monty Crockett, intake supervisor for the Franklin County Juvenile Detention Center, and the world of at-risk teens in Columbus, the sixteenth largest city in America.

Monty had met a lot of people with good intentions over the

years. Past experience has taught him to keep his expectations low and put every newcomer on a short leash. They were normally gone within weeks.

It didn't matter that I arrived with letters of recommendation from court officials and judiciary leaders in Denver. Monty didn't need another failed attempt to help troubled kids who were already losing at life.

It was 1981, and I was beginning the YFC/Youth Guidance program. In early 1982, I moved to a house in the top crime neighborhood in Columbus. Rita and I were married in August, and she joined me there.

While I recruited and trained volunteers and staff and developed programs to meet the growing demands of court-referred kids, Rita reached out to many of the girls in our neighborhood: Tisha, Jackie, Adjowa, Shannon, Priscilla, Carmen, and Anissa.

She was white; they were black.

There were questioning glances from neighbors and unreturned phone calls to minority pastors. There were many walls to take down and many bridges to build. This was slow, discouraging, uphill work. It wasn't enough to succeed with school, social service, and law enforcement officials; we also needed to succeed with parents, pastors, neighbors, and kids on the street.

We would be tried and proved, or found wanting.

We had to be more than people who were there to help the less fortunate and the disadvantaged. We had to establish that we didn't just walk the streets, but we were part of the community. We experienced or witnessed break-ins, burglaries, carjackings, drug overdoses, gunshots—and the births of our two daughters.

Edward was the second teen that Monty referred to me. We became close, and his sisters, mom, and dad became family to us.

His younger sister's birthday was the same as mine, and I had my first birthday dinner in Columbus in their home.

Edward was also my first casualty. His life was a laundry list of conflict. He assaulted his sister and was taken to the hospital with swollen eyes and a fractured cheekbone following an after-school fight. In bitterness, he yelled at me, "My life has been this way for fifteen years; it's not going to change now!" Finally, his life was summed up in the following newspaper report:

STUDENT FATALLY KNIFED IN DISPUTE

A 17-year-old . . . high school student was stabbed to death following an argument. . . . Edward . . . died about 4:30 p.m. after he was knifed in the back. Larry . . . , 14, has been charged with a delinquency charge of murder.[1]

It was a senseless fight gone bad, over shoelaces and sunglasses. It was the end of a young life, a devastating loss for his family, a personal loss for Rita and me, and a setback for Youth Guidance.

Were we winning or losing? Although we were often asked that question, it wasn't about winning or losing. Redemptive action is never about success or failure. It was about consecrated obedience to God, offering help, hope, and truth to the hurting kids and families that lived right around us.

As we grieved the loss of what could have been, we embraced what had come to be. Four years after Rita first walked into the inner city, a fledgling outreach to seven girls had begun to yield the fruit of transformation. Her girls, and those of other staff and volunteers, were now bringing their friends for help. Jan was seventeen, five months pregnant, afraid, alone, alienated from her family, and eighteen hours short of an abortion.

Her mind was made up: "Too many strings come with a baby."

And yet she wanted to talk. The conversation lasted for four and a half hours. For four hours and twenty minutes, her resolve was firm: "I have only one choice: abortion." But something happened in the last ten minutes that changed her heart. Death was changed to life as Jan chose to keep her unborn child. It was extremely difficult for her, but she knew that it was the right choice.

A doctor and an attorney stepped in to handle the adoption procedures and cover the legal and medical costs. An adoptive family was found for the baby, and a tutor guided Jan through her senior year so that she could graduate with her class. A family, supported by their church, opened their home to provide a place for her to live while she healed from the emotional scars of this experience. Two lives were saved that night. The baby was given the gift of life, and Jan was set free from the trauma and bondage that comes with abortion. She was free to receive the love and support she needed for the difficult months ahead.

Faith is a team sport that requires unity in community.

I led the way by living in the inner city and reaching out to juvenile offenders. Rita reached out to girls. Volunteers, staff, and churches came on board. Our girls invited their friends to take the help they needed. An attorney, physician, tutor, adoptive family, host family, and church all joined hands for the sake of a single teenage girl and her unborn child. Through Jesus and the church, you and I have the power to change the direction of individual lives.

Is it possible that God can use what I do here and what you do there to change civilization? Do we have the talent, gifts, abilities, and power to change social, economic, and political systems? Can we possibly transform the development, character, and future of culture?

It seems beyond reach, beyond imagination, but Pope John Paul II thought that we had that power. In one of his most compelling statements, he said, "Be not afraid! Open up, no; swing wide the gates to Christ. Open up to his saving power the confines of the state. Open up economic and political systems. Open up the vast empires of culture, civilization, and development. Be not afraid!"[2]

What does it mean to transform culture?

The word *transform* means to change the character or nature of something.

Culture can be defined as the beliefs, behaviors, customs, and institutions of a given set of people at a given point in time. We have been endowed by God with the ability and the power to change the character and nature of the beliefs, behaviors, customs, and institutions of the people in the world in which we live. When people change, their beliefs, behaviors, customs, and institutions also change.

When the people of God live in unity and community, transforming the world into the likeness of Christ is not just a possibility. It is what God expects of his people. We are to make the common uncommon, the uncertain certain, the natural supernatural, and the temporal eternal. If you profess belief in the God-Man Jesus, who entered our world through a virgin's womb and left it through an empty tomb, how could you do anything less?

Three foundational principles, which we will see in the next few chapters, can help you build your life and transform the culture in which you live. They bring extraordinary power to ordinary people. The first is this:

You must step into your authority . . . through the transforming power of redemptive action.

Jesus said, "All authority in heaven and on earth has been given to me. Therefore go . . ." (Matthew 28:18-19). God gave us authority to perform his work through Jesus Christ, and God dwells in us in the person of the Holy Spirit. We must believe that he did this for us and take steps of faith to bring this promise into daily reality.

God gave authority to you and to me. Authority is "the power of one whose will and commands must be obeyed by others." We must live in that authority and manifest it through the redemptive actions of our lives. These actions ransom, rescue, and set people free from mental, physical, emotional, spiritual, economic, and relational slavery. God reminds us that

> He has rescued us from the dominion of darkness and brought us into the kingdom of the Son he loves, in whom we have redemption, the forgiveness of sins. He is the image of the invisible God, the firstborn over all creation. For by him all things were created: things in heaven and on earth, visible and invisible, whether thrones or powers or rulers or authorities; all things were created by him and for him. He is before all things, and in him all things hold together. And he is the head of the body, the church; he is the beginning and the firstborn from among the dead, so that in everything he might have the supremacy. For God was pleased to have all his fullness dwell in him, and through him to reconcile to himself all things, whether things on earth or things in heaven, by making peace through his blood, shed on the cross. (Colossians 1:13-20)

"All things" includes your boss, addictions, children, failures, spouse, fears, neighborhood, mayor, president, terrorists, Satan, demons, and the principalities of the spirit world. We are either powerful or powerless. We are changing our world or we are not. Too many of us, for too long, have not done so, and you and I are the only ones who can turn that around.

What will you do?

In his book *America's Only Hope,* pastor Tony Evans states, "The church's inability to function as it should can be summed up in its failure to properly respond to Christ's authority."[3]

Dr. Evans reminds us that Jesus is our authority and that for too long we have failed to step into and live in his authority. We have filled our days and weeks with good things while leaving little room for greatness. We take food and blankets to the homeless living under the bridge downtown, but we never consider how to extract them from their lives of futility and want.

If we are followers of Jesus, we carry his authority within us. He has equipped us with every power at his disposal to fulfill his purposes in the world. We have the solutions to poverty, hate, divorce, racism, and greed, but it will cost us something to offer them to the world. If it doesn't cost us anything . . . then it's not a solution.

I believe that God offered mankind the ultimate solution when he sent Jesus into the world to show us the way to God. That solution cost God something. It cost him the life of his Son.

If Jesus is my example, then I need to follow in his steps. When I do, it costs me something. When I travel to the Dominican Republic to visit children and families there, and to assist in the completion of a water purification plant, it costs me something. It costs me time, money, comfort, sweat, aching muscles, skinned knuckles, and separation from my family in a land where I don't speak the language.

But unless we're willing for it to cost us something, the water purification system will not be built, and we will not have a significant impact on the health of those thousands of people. Real solutions never come for free. Every good work has a price tag.

You and I are the doorways through which others pass on their way to redemption, reconciliation, restoration, and transformation. Is your doorway under the authority of Jesus Christ? God offers you and me to the world, which includes taking our authority into the public square.

It's a grand understatement to say that we live in a politically charged world. Religious and political rhetoric are in full swing. What role are we to play in this bitterly contentious arena? In his book *God's Politics: Why the Right Gets It Wrong and the Left Doesn't Get It,* Jim Wallis offers compelling food for thought. He reminds us that our faith has been "co-opted by the Right, and dismissed by the Left."

> It is indeed time to take back our faith. Take back our faith from whom? To be honest, the confusion comes from many sources. From religious right-wingers who claim to know God's political views on every issue, then ignore the subjects that God seems to care the most about. From pedophile priests and cover-up bishops who destroy lives and shame the church. From television preachers whose extravagant lifestyles and crass fund-raising tactics embarrass more Christians than they know. From liberal secularists who want to banish faith from public life and deny spiritual values to the soul of politics. And even from liberal theologians whose cultural confor-

mity and creedal modernity . . . erode the foundations of
biblical faith. From New Age philosophers who want to
make Jesus into a nonthreatening guru. And from politicians who love to say how religious they are but utterly
fail to apply the values of faith to their public leadership
and political policies.[4]

Just as we carry the imperative to get Jesus out into the streets,
we carry the imperative to get Jesus out of partisan politics. He
should not be a manipulative tool in the hands of mockers and
fools.

The voice of Christ should be preached so loudly by our lives
that the counterfeits so poignantly identified by Jim Wallis will
evaporate in the wake of our works. Our God is the God of the
poor and the oppressed, not the God of political party platforms.
Our lives should render the counterfeit, manipulative, political,
and prosperous Christ . . . dead and gone!

Poverty and homosexual marriage . . .

National defense and the environment . . .

Abortion and welfare . . .

Economic justice and religious freedom . . .

Truth and compassion . . .

are all religious issues.

All are issues for the good of humanity, and none is the property
of a single political party, Right or Left. If this is true, then what

are you doing to change that equation? What will you do today in small, quiet, meaningful ways to change the world forever?

We are here to create culture as a foretaste of what is to come. I believe that one day we will have an opportunity to walk with God in a kingdom of peace. That is the culture to come. In the meantime, our work is to seek that kind of kingdom for the world where we live today. Our lives should be such that they influence the beliefs, behaviors, and customs right here and now, so that our world increasingly reflects the character and nature of God.

When you step into your authority and release the transforming power of redemptive action, you will do what you say you believe by addressing causes, not just symptoms, and by providing alternatives.

REFLECTIONS

Seek God and ask him what you should do. I am not going to create a checklist to guide you to some predetermined course of action. Instead, reflect on this section and let God direct you to where he wants you to go.

I have often been led to do something that no one else was doing. It got me out of the comfort zone of simply being part of a committee; it met real and immediate needs, caused me to rely on God, and pushed me to invite others to join in the mission.

How will you step into your authority?

What will your redemptive action look like?

THE POWER OF ONENESS

SETTING PEOPLE FREE THROUGH RECONCILING RELATIONSHIPS

We and God have business with each other through the Spirit and in opening ourselves to God and each other, our deepest destiny is fulfilled.

—WILLIAM JAMES

SOMETHING SPECIAL HAPPENS when people come together in unity and community to pursue a common cause or pray for a common need. God blesses the people and the process. When we are reconciled with one another, a power emerges from our being together as one. Our second principle for building your life and transforming your culture reflects that.

You must model the power of oneness . . . through reconciling relationships that set people free.

Whether you think of Bono primarily as a rock star, AIDS activist, Nobel Peace Prize nominee, cryptic lyricist, or a radical, countercultural Christian, he certainly understands the power of one, as he so vividly presents in the lyrics to the song "One," which reminds us that the source of all unity is love, and that love leaves us if it is not used. When we submit ourselves to God and align our desires with his, we find that we are able to align ourselves with other people, as well. Bono challenges us to use the strength of our differences to help one another. My strength should be used where you are weak, and your strength should be used where I am weak. As we "carry each other," we get to share in the oneness that can only be found by giving ourselves away to each other. No, we're not exactly the same, but it's that diversity that God uses to make the world a better place.

The oneness of life that we model through Jesus identifies us as brothers, sisters, husbands and wives, family, and church. By our carrying one another in unconditional love, the power of Jesus is released into the world.

My friend Dan Brake offers these thoughts on "One." Do they resonate with you?

1. Husband and wife are one life, but not the same. They carry each other.

2. The body of Christ is one body with many parts. We each play a role, and a body works well when the independent parts move in harmony. The parts carry each other.

3. Jesus is one man, one life, one love, one blood that paid the ultimate price for all who believe. He carries and sustains

us. Now we do what we should, not because we are bound by the law, but because we adore and love him.

Our oneness draws the world to us, as others see something that they want and need. It's winsome and inviting because God dwells with us. This isn't spiritual porridge, but spiritual truth.

Our God is personal yet eternal, reachable yet beyond reach, here and everywhere. His redemptive power transforms us through unity, community, and wholeness.

> I will dwell among the Israelites and be their God. They will know that I am the LORD their God, who brought them out of Egypt so that I might dwell among them. I am the LORD their God. (Exodus 29:45-46)

> The Word became flesh and made his dwelling among us. (John 1:14)

God has "pitched his tent" in us and among us.

Where God is, there is peace, calm, protection, hope, comfort, rest, wholeness, love, and mercy. Are you where God is? Do others see God in you? Does your life attract others who are seeking what you have? We are drawn to God, and the world is drawn to him through us. His dwelling among us is revealed in our oneness.

> *Our oneness is modeled and released when . . .*
> *We pursue repentance, not satisfaction*
> *We worship God, not his creation*
> *We seek holiness, not acceptance*
> *We make disciples, not converts*

We value life, not convenience
We seek truth, not compliance
We model love, not tolerance
We want less, not more
We seek mercy with justice
We seek God, not only his gifts
We seek significance, not success
We prioritize family, not career
We give without expecting a return
We collaborate without competing
We pursue the cross, not the crowns
We value community with diversity
We seek to serve before being served
We pursue justice, not self-justification
We speak the truth in love, not just to be loved
We look to the needs of others, not just our own
We live in community and abandon individualism
We embrace biblical orthodoxy, not situational ethics
We embrace economic justice as readily as social justice
We model the law of love instead of the law of retribution
We become the voice of the poor, not of the privileged
We empower people to change; we don't imprison
* them with entitlements*
We are known for our love one for another
We turn the other cheek
We follow in his steps
We confess our sins.

Cultural transformation occurs when followers of Jesus do what comes naturally. This happens when we live in right relationship with the world and allow them to taste our salt and see our light.

It's daily and routine, not dramatic.

It's ordinary, but it becomes extraordinary when we allow God to touch it.

When we model the power of oneness through reconciling relationships, we will transform the world in which we live.

In the previous chapter, I introduced you to Jan. We rescued and restored Jan and her unborn child through the power of oneness and the reconciling relationships she experienced in the Youth Guidance program. Jan and her child were but two lives that were spared, and yet that pioneering effort in inner city Columbus in the early days of the 1980s has become a powerful force for cultural transformation.

When I left, we had a handful of staff and volunteers.

Now, twenty-five years later, under the leadership of Scott Arnold, the YFC/Youth Guidance program has become a major source of renewal in the inner city. In the last two years, they have received national recognition for their work and government grants in excess of one million dollars.

Through mentoring, tutoring, and life skills programs, there were significant reductions in youth crime and school dropout rates. Last year, 150 students participated in the program. Ninety-three percent of the participants remained in school or took on full-time employment, and 95 percent stayed out of trouble with the juvenile justice system. These results were achieved at the modest budget of $160 per student.

YFC/Youth Guidance now operates in seven central Ohio counties. It serves 3,500 to 4,000 individuals and families a year through collaborative efforts with detention centers, churches, and local agencies.

I had no idea what God had in mind when I rolled into town pulling a small trailer behind my VW in the early summer of 1981. I had no concept of the power of oneness that God places within reconciling relationships. I'm amazed at what he has done.

I simply started with the small, the lost, the lonely, and the "least of these."

God and many others did the rest.

REFLECTIONS

What does "oneness" look like?

ACTIONS

Identify one social problem that burdens you deeply. Pray about it. Write what you intend to do about it.

Identify at least two other people you will ask to help you. Pray about it. Go ask them to help.

Together, identify the resources necessary to provide a lasting impact. Pray about it. Go recruit the resources.

Go do it.

THE KINGDOM OF GOD

RESTORING PEOPLE TO GOD AND THE WORLD

The holiest moment of the church service is the moment when God's people—strengthened by preaching and sacrament—go out of the church door into the world to be the Church. We don't go to church; we are the church.

—ERNEST SOUTHCOTT

WITH POWERFUL DIRECTNESS, Jesus says, "The kingdom of God is within you" (Luke 17:21). This is a statement of fact, a living reality that is never in doubt, and it points us toward our third principle.

You must pursue the kingdom of God . . . by restoring people to God and the world he created.

God resides in us as we follow Jesus.

What does this mean? What is the kingdom of God, and why did Jesus say so much about it?

The kingdom of God is characterized by his reign and his dominion.

The kingdom of God is a kingdom of love and is filled with peace.

It's a difficult concept to describe or fully understand. Scripture tells us that this is a kingdom of righteousness, joy, and peace, but it's not a physical location that carries a zip code (Romans 14:17). It cannot be touched or seen, but it can be tasted.

> "The kingdom of God is not a matter of talk but of power." (1 Corinthians 4:20)

We cannot hear it with our ears, but it is powerful and can be experienced. It cannot be seen, yet it cannot be shaken (Hebrews 12:28).

In short, God's kingdom is God's rule, dominion, power, and authority. It's the reign of God. It's his everlasting dominion from generation to generation throughout all time, matter, creation, principalities, and powers. It is tasted in righteousness, peace, and joy. It is invisible, but all-powerful. It's where God resides and reigns in the world and within his followers.

Since our rebellion against God (Genesis 1–2), God has been working throughout history to reestablish his dominion and authority (his kingdom rule). He has given us prophets, priests, kings, the Ten Commandments, Jesus, and the Holy Spirit to communicate his truth to us. Each has helped to reestablish God's authority since the early days of the Garden of Eden.

God has added one more person to that list—he has added you.

He "has made us to be a kingdom and priests to serve his God and Father" (Revelation 1:6). What are we to do with this glorious and awful truth?

It is an "awful truth" because there is a battle for human souls. The kingdom of God and the kingdom of Satan are at war. We are citizens of God's kingdom or we are citizens of Satan's domain. "He who is not with me is against me, and he who does not gather with me, scatters" (Luke 11:23).

"If anyone's name was not found written in the book of life, he was thrown into the lake of fire" (Revelation 20:15). In this war, there are no bystanders, no conscientious objectors, and no neutral ground. We are with Christ or against him. The awful truth will be revealed when Christ returns to judge the world.

The 2003 Album of the Year was Johnny Cash's *American IV: The Man Comes Around.* The title track is a haunting portrayal of the end of time when Jesus ("The Man") returns ("comes around") in judgment to crush Satan, destroy his demons, and imprison his followers.

The backdrop to the song can be found in the book of Revelation:

> I saw heaven standing open and there before me was a white horse, whose rider is called Faithful and True. With justice he judges and makes war. His eyes are like blazing fire, and on his head are many crowns. Out of his mouth comes a sharp sword with which to strike down the nations. . . . He treads the winepress of the fury of the wrath of God Almighty. (Revelation 19:11-12, 15)

The song conveys the chilling will of God to choose whom he will to join in his kingdom of peace, and to choose as he may those doomed to eternal despair. It reveals the terror of all who face their fate apart from God, and the reward of all who have yielded their will, their allegiance, and their lives to God and his purposes.

The song reminds us that God is Alpha and Omega, the beginning and the end, "who is, and who was, and who is to come, the Almighty" (Revelation 1:8). It also reminds us that we play a critical role in our own destiny, a role that should never be taken lightly. "Behold, I am coming soon! My reward is with me, and I will give to everyone according to what he has done" (Revelation 22:12).

What a chilling reminder of the awful truth of God's wrath and judgment that will fall on all humankind. What a terrible burden you and I bear to tell this story to the world. God is merciful, true, and loving, and he is undeniably a God of judgment. "And the devil, who deceived them, was thrown in the lake of burning sulfur, where the beast and the false prophet had been thrown. They will be tormented day and night for ever and ever" (Revelation 20:10).

Where will you stand on the day of God's wrath?

On whose side do you stand in the battle for your soul?

Do you love God enough to share this message with your world?

Is there someone you need to tell?

Does someone you know need to be restored to God?

I've shared the awful truth about the kingdom of God. Let me now share the glorious truth by telling one final story.

On Christmas 1914, soldiers had drawn their battle lines in Flanders along the borders of Belgium and France. British, French, and Belgian soldiers were joined by troops from India and Africa, with orders to protect their homeland and that of their allies. Across the battlefield were Germans, Prussians, Saxons, Bavarians, and Westphalians, with orders to kill, conquer, and possess the lands of others.

As in all wars, it was kill or be killed.

Since August, the European front had claimed hundreds of thousands of lives and left many more wounded or missing. An appeal from Pope Benedict XV for a Christmas cease-fire was rejected by both warring factions and became fodder for further sarcasm and cynicism.

An article in *The New Republic* suggested that "the stench of battle should rise above the churches where they preach good-will to men. A few carols, a little incense and some tinsel will heal no wounds. A wartime Christmas would be a festival 'so empty that it jeers at us.'"[1] Though both sides highly regarded the tradition of Christmas, they would continue their fight to the death.

They all faced a Christmas of rain, mud, flooded trenches, cold rations, and the stench of floating, decomposing bodies. Many were forced to sleep upright for fear of drowning in their foxholes or their protective trenches in the swampland. At times, the lines were just sixty yards from the enemy—so close that they would throw weighted newspapers or rations to one another.

On the morning of December 19, a most extraordinary thing happened. Some Germans dropped their weapons, raised their arms, and came out to take in their wounded, followed by the English and French, who reclaimed their own. The Germans then beckoned the allies to come and talk with them, and soon they were sharing meals and stories.

The Germans had brought Christmas trees to the front lines with which to celebrate the holiday, and the British had sweets, pipe tobacco, and a greeting card from the king. Upon returning to their fortified battle positions that evening, the Germans proposed a concert in honor of their captain's birthday.

They invited the British to attend, provided that they agree to suspend all hostilities between 7:30 and 8:30 P.M. This they did, and at the appointed hour all heads were lifted safely in sight of the enemy. What began as a point of close deadly contact and conflict turned into a Christmas Eve truce just days later that extended for miles in both directions.

The rain gave way to cold, clear skies and a brightly shining moon. They sang Christmas carols that boomed across the battlefield for the enemy's benefit. The soldiers left their guns behind as they met in No Man's Land to share gifts and prayers. Lighted Christmas trees appeared out of nowhere. The battle had ceased. The combatants had submitted to a higher authority that recognized in one another the very reason that Jesus, the Christ child, was born.

Their actions gave evidence of a higher power and authority, a foretaste of what we will one day experience.

> A sudden friendship had been struck up, the truce of God had been called, and for the rest of Christmas day, not a shot was fired along our section. The chaplain and the German *Oberstleutnant* settled upon a joint service in No Man's Land. Adams would open with the 23rd Psalm, and prayers would follow from both sides in English and German. Intermingled, the dead lay in the sixty yards between their lines. Soldiers went out to identify the bodies, carrying the Germans to one side, the British to the other. Before the sun was high, the digging had begun. The British brought over wooden crosses made from biscuit boxes for both sides. If the shooting

resumed, they would be contending through the crosses and the graves.[2]

The cease-fire did not last, of course. In the end, the governments sent in fresh troops that were not "compromised" by the fraternization of the Christmas truce. It was not "reasonable" to pursue peace, because the French and Belgians were unwilling to give up lost homeland and the Germans would not willingly give back conquered territory. It didn't matter what the men in the trenches thought. They were there to win or die trying.

What if the war had ended with the Christmas truce?

For one thing, the world would not have lost six thousand people every day for forty-six months. Stability, restoration, free trade, economic growth, peace, and prosperity would have been given an opportunity to grow from the soil of peace. Instead, the British leaders ordered a continual military bombardment on Christmas Eve so that the truce could not be resumed.

When the soldiers submitted to God's authority, they erased battle lines, buried and mourned their dead, worshiped God, celebrated life, and let faith rule the day. For a brief interval amidst the destruction and desolation of war, thousands of soldiers experienced a small taste of God's kingdom. We know in part what they experienced, and someday we will know fully. God intends for us to bring this peace to the world. When we do, in one life or in the lives of many, we restore people to God and his world through the power of his kingdom.

The kingdom of God exists because God reigns. Our part is to bring our lives under his sovereign will. In other words, the glorious truth about the kingdom of God is that we worship a living, loving, personal, all-powerful King who allows us to taste his presence as we await his return to take us home with him for eternity.

This glorious news is what we all want, hope for, and will some day have when the kingdom of God is released in us and we use its restorative power to bring people to God.

The kingdom of God . . .

Has come. "The kingdom of God has come upon you." (Matthew 12:28)

Is available to all. "God so loved the world that he gave his one and only Son, that whoever believes in him shall not perish but have eternal life." (John 3:16)

Brings forgiveness of sins. "Repent, for the kingdom of heaven is near." (Matthew 3:2)

"He has rescued us from the dominion of darkness and brought us into the kingdom of the Son he loves, in whom we have redemption, the forgiveness of sins." (Colossians 1:13-14)

Can be found by a child. "I tell you the truth, unless you change and become like little children, you will never enter the kingdom of heaven." (Matthew 18:3)

Gives you value. "He who is least in the kingdom of heaven is greater than [John the Baptist]." (Matthew 11:11)

Gives you authority. "I will give you the keys of the kingdom of heaven; whatever you bind on earth will be bound in heaven, and whatever you loose on earth will be loosed in heaven." (Matthew 16:19)

Has defeated Satan. "I saw Satan fall like lightning from heaven." (Luke 10:18)

"The accuser of our brothers, who accuses them before our God day and night, has been hurled down." (Revelation 12:10)

Is accompanied by healing and deliverance. "The blind receive sight, the lame walk, those who have leprosy are cured, the deaf hear, the dead are raised, and the good news is preached to the poor." (Matthew 11:5)

Is a kingdom of mercy. "The servant's master took pity on him, canceled the debt and let him go." (Matthew 18:27)

Cannot be thwarted. "This gospel of the kingdom will be preached in the whole world as a testimony to all nations, and then the end will come." (Matthew 24:14)

Is your inheritance. "Then the King will say to those on his right, 'Come, you who are blessed by my Father; take your inheritance, the kingdom prepared for you since the creation of the world." (Matthew 25:34)

When we embrace the truth of God's kingdom, it reaches through our everyday, ordinary lives and empowers us to change the world. To me, that is the power of an ordinary life—the transforming impact of redemptive action.

∾

I wrote this book because I was unable not to write it. I wrote out of the brokenness and the fullness of my own ordinary life in the hopes that I could help *you* believe that *your* ordinary life counts, and that *you* can make a difference.

In God's sight, there are no "little people" or "little places." When we live in consecrated moments of obedience to God, he gives us the power to influence our generation.

God calls us to take redemptive action with all that we know about God and ourselves by creating reconciling relationships with others. This will set them free to be restored to God and the world in which they live, transforming that world into the likeness of Jesus Christ.

Can we change the world forever? Yes. There is power in an ordinary life. Together, you and God are extraordinary!

> *You are a letter from Christ . . .*
> *Written not with ink but with the Spirit of the living God,*
> *Not on tablets of stone but on tablets of human hearts. . . .*
> *Our competence comes from God.*
> *He has made us competent as ministers of a new covenant—*
> *Not of the letter but of the Spirit;*
> *For the letter kills, but the Spirit gives life.*
>
> 2 CORINTHIANS 3:3-6

REFLECTIONS

What will you do with "the Kingdom of God that is in you"?

What would a transformed world look like?

Epilogue

CIELO:
HEAVEN ON EARTH

EPILOGUES ARE CLOSING sections in which authors provide concluding commentary. It's the author's last word. But I see this section as more of a beginning, a prologue or preview of coming attractions.

I just boarded American Airlines flight 882 in Santo Domingo, Dominican Republic, and in a moment we'll be lifting off for Miami. It's 1:59 P.M. on Sunday, April 30, 2006, and I've just spent seven days in heaven alongside thirty-nine other men from the United States.

When I left Columbus on April 23, I was the husband of one wife and the father of two daughters. Today, as I return home, I am still the husband of one wife, but I have brought an additional eight children for Rita and me to love and care for. We added six sisters (*hermanas*), Karina, Jasmine, Angela, Viviana, Lisette, and Lizimar, and two brothers (*hermanos*), Coli and Miguel, to our current two-girl crew of Rebecca and Rachel. We still haven't figured out what all of this means, but something very special happened in the D.R.—something of God.

I went to the D.R. with Brent Markley and thirty-eight others on a mission trip sponsored by Mission Emanuel, which operates under the auspices of The Gathering. It was my first third-world mission experience, and I don't speak Spanish.

We went to build and reconstruct homes in two impoverished communities, Cielo and Nazaret, on the outskirts of Santo Domingo. At least, that's what they told us. In hindsight, it was a "bait and switch," in the very best of ways.

We worked hard in the ninety-five-degree heat. We mixed cement by hand, carried concrete blocks up and down hills, replaced dirt floors with concrete, installed an indoor bathroom, put roofs on homes, and painted a house. The "bait" was the work we went to do. The "switch" came when we met, served, and loved the men, women, and children of Cielo and Nazaret.

Cielo is Spanish for "heaven."

If you were to join me on a walk through the streets and alleys of Cielo, you might conclude that it was anything but heaven. Houses are constructed of poorly-made cement blocks, discarded sheet metal, and plywood or wood pallets that have been broken apart and nailed together to build the walls of houses. Many homes have dirt floors and no plumbing.

When it rains, the main street fills with water that runs down the side streets and alleys to pour into homes and turn living room and bedroom floors into mud and muck. When morning comes and the streets are dried by the hot sun, you will find human feces on the streets, flushed out of their inadequate waste removal system. When the average family lives on six dollars a day, you can't expect it to be otherwise. However, in the midst of rain, heat, poverty, need, want, and hard work, we discovered a community of hope, faith, love, and family.

As the forty members of our group, adults of all shapes and sizes, headed out to our daily work sites, we were greeted by a chorus of children's voices calling, "Americano! Americano! Chiclet? Chiclet?" Barefoot boys and girls, as well as those in freshly washed jeans or school uniforms, asked us for gum and candy, or took our hands and silently walked with us. Although our hands were dirty and sweaty, there was always a little person attached.

Day One. I meekly tested my assortment of smiles, nods, winks, and hand signals, a few *Holas* and *Biens,* and an occasional *Gracias* or *Buenos Dias.* Thank goodness, Rebecca and Rachel weren't there to critique my awkward but heartfelt Spanglish!

Day Two. Karina, all smiles at age seven, the only child of a single mom, adopted me, and I picked up her cousins Jasmine and Coli in a three-kid package deal. When they weren't in school, they were stuck to me like glue, not far from mom's watchful eye. During lunch, I selected a child from a long list for Rita and me to sponsor in attending the Cielo school. Our small monthly gift buys her education materials, school uniform, and one meal a day. After lunch, I met Luz Angela, a timid, quiet second grader that we now sponsor. After several photographs and at least two tickles, she finally managed a smile. Day two ended with a community dinner and service for 248 men during pelting rain and lightning flashes.

Day Three. I toured the Nazaret School, begun by Rosario and Javier De La Cruz in a single room. The Cielo and Nazaret schools now educate six hundred children annually.

I concluded the tour and sat down in a breezeway, where I was joined by eight-year-old Viviana. She smiled broadly at me, and we were immediate friends. I met her mom, who works at the school, and we parted with a hug. Viviana, her two sisters, one brother, mom, and dad had just become part of the growing extended Hook family.

Day Three concluded with a worship service at the Mission Emanuel youth center. I borrowed Brent's cell phone and slipped out back to call Rita as the room filled up with various shades of white-, brown-, and black-skinned people. I returned to the singing in English and Spanish, and to children moving about among Dominican, American, and Haitian laps.

It didn't seem to matter that a few Americanos were blowing soap bubbles for four-year-old children or speaking quietly with them in the midst of worship. Actually, it all seemed to be part of the worship. Three minutes later, Karina appeared from nowhere and sat in my lap. Two minutes passed, and Viviana was sitting by my side. How and why they found me I do not know.

And then the tears began to flow . . . as they do now.

This was it. This was Cielo. This was heaven.

I was 2,500 miles from home, related to no one by blood, and yet I was with family. I was with God's people and in his presence. In Cielo, a community synonymous with poverty and want, various mixed races, skin colors, and languages had somehow become one. We talked, sang, clapped, prayed, worshiped, and hugged, and as we did so, all the voices, languages, skin colors, and social classes blended into one. In those moments, there was no want or need, but wholeness and joy. It was a rare and precious gift of God.

By night's end, Karina was fast asleep on my lap, her head tucked under my sweaty chin and my work-weary right arm muscles, sore from preventing her from falling. Just before Viviana fell asleep with her head resting on my left arm, she reached up, touched my face with her hand, and wiped several beads of sweat from my forehead with her fingers.

It was the touch of God. He was in the house and we were God's family. We were Shalom. We experienced what I thought had been reserved for heaven.

I so wanted Rita, Rebecca, and Rachel there to share in that moment.

Day Four. We visited a leprosarium in the morning and left, having been encouraged by the residents. A blind leper woman with one arm was confined to a wheelchair; she prayed for one of our men. We left with no reasons to complain ever again and spent the afternoon participating in a pick-up baseball game, coloring with some kids, reading to others, or buying Pepsi Blue. Two kids walked into the store with us and seven others managed to wriggle into the group by the time we got to the cashier.

Day Five. We finished our work projects and held a dedication service for all the homes we renovated or constructed. This time the tears were theirs—tears of happiness in receiving our gifts of work and service. We smiled, and some of us cried as one grateful mom covered her face with her shirt to hide the embarrassment of her tears. We weren't finished yet.

Days Six and Seven. We packed up forty Dominican men and took them to a hotel on the ocean for a two-day retreat in preparation for their coming leadership roles in their families, community, and churches.

Today is Day Eight. I'm now en route from Miami to Columbus, and I can't wait to return in October. When I do, Rita and others will be going with me.

When I reflect on this week, I realize that there are really only three differences between you, me, and our Dominican and Haitian brothers, sisters, and children in Cielo and Nazaret:

1. They are there and we are here.

2. They have abundant joy and few opportunities.

3. We have abundant opportunities and comparatively little joy.

In our world, kids play with balls, bats, helmets, uniforms, and manicured baseball diamonds. In the world I visited, kids play with sticks and bottle caps using a home plate painted on the road where two streets connect. In our world, we keep a safe and guarded distance from one another. In their world, sweaty people hold hands, wipe sweat from one another's arms and faces, and hug one another. They have something we are missing.

Will you join me in Cielo? Will you come with me to Nazaret?

For the past ten years, Jack Larson has led the efforts of The Gathering in transforming these two small communities through Mission Emanuel. We have seen two schools, medical and dental clinics, and a youth center rise up from the ground. We have seen homes built, lives restored, churches growing, and marriages transformed. Sixty-five nationals now run the ministry on a daily basis, but we have just begun.

There are approximately two thousand families living in Cielo and Nazaret. Will you join Jack, Rosario, Javier, myself, and the many people who gather here each year? Will you take the principles of this book and focus them for just one week with me in the Dominican Republic?

Will you add your ordinary life to mine so that together we can create something extraordinary? What if hundreds just like you—ordinary people—joined this effort?

Don't you believe that in twenty years, through our efforts and God's grace, we could leave the legacy of a transformed Cielo and Nazaret?

Visit www.TheGathering.org, or write to Jack Larson at www.MissionEmanuel.org, to ask how you can serve. Contact me at www.GatheringColumbus.com and let me know when you are coming. Hopefully, by then, I'll have learned the language!

One final thought . . .

In Cielo and Nazaret, the streets have no names. On my walk from Nazaret to Cielo, I saw one bent street sign along the way. The road that took me from Nazaret (Nazareth) to Cielo (Heaven) was called Jerusalen (Jerusalem). For Jesus, there was only one road from his childhood home of Nazareth that he could take to heaven, and it was the road that passed through Jerusalem and up to a lonely hill with a cross at the top.

Jesus took the road of redemptive action for you, for me, and for the world.

Will you join me on the road called Jerusalen that passes between Nazaret and Cielo? The rest of your life's story has yet to be written. Will you write just one chapter with me, in two small villages where the streets have no name? Rita and I will be there to greet you.

After all, we have family there . . . and so do you.

Notes

CHAPTER 1: *You Can Make a Difference*

1. Dirk Johnson, "In Georgia, a Matter of Faith: How a hostage's own struggles aided justice," *Newsweek,* March 28, 2006, www.msnbc.msn.com/id/7244880/site/newsweek.

2. Rick Warren, *The Purpose Driven Life* (Grand Rapids: Zondervan, 2002), 257-258.

3. "Ex-hostage: 'I wanted to gain his trust,'" transcript of Ashley Smith's statement to the press, *CNN,* March 14, 2005, www.cnn.com/2005/LAW/03/14/smith.transcript.

4. Ibid.

5. Ashley Smith, *Unlikely Angel: The Untold Story of the Atlanta Hostage Hero* (Grand Rapids: Zondervan, 2005), 61-62, 83-101.

CHAPTER 2: *No Little People*

1. Francis A. Schaeffer, *No Little People* (Downers Grove, Ill.: InterVarsity, 1974), 13.

2. Ibid.

3. Charles Colson, *Against the Night,* (Ann Arbor, Mich.: Servant, 1989), 57.

4. Neelesh Misra, "Knowledge of Nature May Have Saved Tribes," *The Columbus Dispatch,* January 5, 2005.

5. Frank S. Mead, ed., *Encyclopedia of Religious Quotations,* (Westwood, N.J.: Revell, 1965), 126.

CHAPTER 3: *The Path Less Taken*

1. Michka Assayas, *Bono* (New York: Riverhead, 2005), 321.

CHAPTER 4: *Chosen by God*

1. C. Everett Koop and Francis A. Schaeffer, *Whatever Happened to the Human Race?* rev. ed. (Westchester, Ill.: Crossway, 1983), 79-80. Italics, brackets, and parentheses are in the original.

2. Bill and Kathy Peel, *Discover Your Destiny* (Colorado Springs: NavPress, 1996), 31.

3. Oswald Chambers, *My Utmost for His Highest* (New York: Dodd Mead, 1935), 246, 262.

CHAPTER 5: *Partnering with God*

1. Elizabeth Dole, from her keynote address at The Gathering breakfast, November 2, 1994, Columbus, Ohio.

2. Elisabeth Elliot, *Through Gates of Splendor* (Wheaton, Ill.: Tyndale, 1984), 189.

3. Ibid., 175.

4. Ibid., 194.

5. Rebecca Barnes, "The Rest of the Story," *Christianity Today*, January 2006, 39.

6. Jonathan Cott, *Bob Dylan: The Essential Interviews* (New York: Wenner, 2006), 24.

7. Elisabeth Elliot, *Discipline: The Glad Surrender* (Old Tappan, N.J.: Revell, 1982), 33.

CHAPTER 6: *Completed by God*

1. Viktor E. Frankl, *Man's Search for Meaning* (Boston: Beacon, 2006), 37, 38. Italics are in the original.

2. Philip Yancey, *Reaching for the Invisible God* (Grand Rapids: Zondervan, 2000), 110-111.

3. C. S. Lewis, *Mere Christianity* (New York: Macmillan, 1943), 174.

4. Elisabeth Elliot, quoted in *Pentecostal Evangel*, October 22, 1978, 2.

5. Thomas à Kempis, *The Imitation of Christ* (Milwaukee: Bruce, 1962), 173.

CHAPTER 7: *Can You Hear Me Now?*

1. Beth Nimmo and Darrell Scott with Steve Rabey, *Rachel's Tears* (Nashville: Nelson, 2000), 174.

2. Darrell Scott with Steve Rabey, *Chain Reaction* (Nashville: Nelson, 2001), 22.

CHAPTER 8: *The Still, Small Voice*

1. Richard Foster, *Celebration of Discipline* (San Francisco: Harper & Row, 1978), 13.

2. Jim Towey, from his keynote address at the Ohio Prayer Breakfast, May 1, 2003, Columbus, Ohio.

3. Ibid.

4. Henry Blackaby and Claude King, *Experiencing God* (Nashville: Broadman & Holman, 1994), 84-85.

5. Kathleen Norris, *The Cloister Walk* (New York: Riverhead, 1996), 63.

6. Thomas Merton, *No Man Is an Island* (New York: Harcourt Brace, 1955), 118.

7. Albert Einstein, quoted in Elisabeth Elliot, *Discipline: The Glad Surrender* (Old Tappan, N.J.: Revell, 1982), 32.

CHAPTER 9: *Believing Is Seeing*

1. Matthew Kelly, from his address at the Catholic Men's Conference, Ohio Dominican University, March 12, 2005.

2. Laura Berman Fortgang. *Take Yourself to the Top* (New York: Tarcher/Penguin, 2005), 38.

3. Charles R. Swindoll, *Living Above the Level of Mediocrity* (Waco, Tex.: Word, 1987), 88.

4. Dr. Myles Munroe, conversation with the author, October 30, 2002.

5. See John 11:21-40.

6. David L. Steward with Robert L. Shook, *Doing Business by the Good Book* (New York: Hyperion, 2004), 160.

7. Ibid., 75, 203.

CHAPTER 10: *Strength and Stability*

1. Robert D. Dale, *Keeping the Dream Alive* (Nashville: Broadman, 1988), 17.

2. Digital History, "African American Voices," *Harriet Tubman,* www.digitalhistory.uh.edu/black_voices/voices_display.cfm?id=74.

3. The Harriet Tubman story is compiled from information on the following Internet sites: www.answers.com/topic/harriet-tubman; http://harriettubman.info; and www.pbs.org/wgbh/aia/part4/4p1535.html.

4. http://www.cornerstoneministry.org/magazine/cover_story/coverstory0302.htm

CHAPTER 11: *Why On Earth Am I Here?*

1. Dr. Myles Munroe, conversation with the author, October 30, 2002.

2. Maximilian Kolbe's story is based on information taken from the book *Maximilian Kolbe: Saint of Auschwitz,* by Elaine Murray Stone (Paulist, 1997).

3. http://myhero.com/myhero/hero.asp?hero=mkolbe

4. John Neumann, "Saint Maximilian Kolbe," Slaves of the Immaculate Heart of Mary, www.catholicism.org/pages/maximilian-kolbe.html.

5. Jim Tressel's story was compiled from his keynote address at The Gathering breakfast, March 6, 2003, Columbus, Ohio.

CHAPTER 12: *Mission Possible!*

1. The soldiers' rescue story is based on information taken from the book *Ghost Soldiers* by Hampton Sides (Anchor, 2001).

2. John C. Maxwell, "The 7 Marks of a Mission Minded Man," *New Man* (Jan/Feb 2004): 25.

3. The story of Stylianos Kyriakides is based on information taken from the book *Running with Pheidippides: Stylianos Kyriakides, the Miracle Marathoner* by Nick Tsiotos and Andy Dabilis (Syracuse University Press, 2001).

4. The text of Russ Corley's remarks at Greg Schworm's memorial service were supplied to the author by e-mail.

CHAPTER 13: *"Success" Is Optional*

1. Chris Spielman's story was compiled from his keynote address at the Ohio Prayer Breakfast, May 2, 2002, Columbus, Ohio, and from notes he supplied to the author.

2. Hudson Taylor's story is compiled from information taken from www.wholesomewords.org/missions/biotaylor2.html.

3. Tony Campolo, *Everything You've Heard Is Wrong* (Dallas: Word, 1992), 117-118.

4. Bob Buford, *Half Time* (Grand Rapids: Zondervan, 1994), 153.

CHAPTER 14: *Looking Under the Hood*

1. University of Kentucky, "What Willie Lynch had to say in 1812," AWARE student group, www.uky.edu/StudentOrgs/AWARE/archives/lynch.html.

2. Bill Butterworth, from his keynote address at the Columbus Leadership Prayer Breakfast, October 2, 1991, Columbus, Ohio.

CHAPTER 15: *Nuts and Bolts*

1. Arthur F. Miller and Ralph T. Mattson, *The Truth About You* (Old Tappan, N.J.: Revell, 1977), 32-54.

2. Ben Carson, *Gifted Hands* (Grand Rapids: Zondervan, 1990), 108.

3. Ibid., 56-57.

4. Ibid., 37.

CHAPTER 16: *God Equips the Chosen*

1. David R. Meuse, from his keynote address at The Leadership Forum, September 26, 2003, Columbus, Ohio.

2. Julanne Hohbach, "Band of Brothers," *Columbus CEO* magazine (October 2004), 13.

3. Bono, from his address to the National Prayer Breakfast in Washington, D.C., February 2, 2006; www.data.org/archives/000774.php.

4. Kirsta Niemie, from an e-mail sent to the author, September 9, 2004.

5. George W. Bush, from his keynote address at the 2006 White House National Conference on Faith-Based and Community Initiatives, March 9, 2006, Washington, D.C.

6. Mary H. Cooper, "Lower Vote Turnout," *CQ Researcher* (October 2000).

CHAPTER 17: *Friendship with God*

1. Anthony Breznican, "Ex-con artist sees life flash by," *The Columbus Dispatch*, January 3, 2003, F6.

2. www.kivana.com/acts/FrankAbagnale.html

3. The major elements of the Frank Abagnale Jr. story are based on information taken from a *Focus on the Family* radio broadcast from 1993. An extensive account of Abagnale's story, "Skywayman: The Story of Frank W. Abagnale Jr.," by Rachael Bell, can be found at www.crimelibrary.com/criminal_mind/scams/frank_abagnale/index.html.

4. Breznican.

5. The information in this chapter and the next has been profoundly influenced by the work of John Tulson and Larry Kreider, *The Four Priorities* (Orlando: The Gathering, 2005). See www.the4priorities.com/program/4pcourse.cfm.

6. Michka Assayas, *Bono* (New York: Riverhead, 2005), 204.

7. Johnny Cash, *Cash: The Autobiography* (San Francisco: Harper, 1997), 207.

8. Bobby Bowden's story was compiled from his keynote address at The Gathering breakfast, April 12, 1995, Columbus, Ohio.

CHAPTER 18: *The Next Sacred Priorities*

1. Ken Davis, "The Balanced Life," in *Moving Beyond Belief: A Strategy for Personal Growth* (Nashville: Nelson, 1993), 96.

2. Jay Kesler, "The Church," in *Moving Beyond Belief,* 203-204.

3. The story of Pete Maravich and the two young boys at the six-mile race was recounted by Adolph Coors IV at the Athletic Club of Columbus, October 27, 1989.

CHAPTER 20: *No More New Year's Resolutions!*

1. Jimmy Golen, *"Nothing Tops Red Sox Saga," The Columbus Dispatch,* December 30, 2004.

2. Tom Verducci, "Blood and Guts," *Sports Illustrated* (November 1, 2004).

3. Tim Hansel, *Holy Sweat* (Dallas: Word, 1987), 85.

4. Peter J. Daniels, *How to Reach Your Life Goals* (Unity Park, South Australia: House of Tabor, 1985), 133.

5. Ibid., 133-142.

CHAPTER 21: *Joining Up*

1. Monty Roberts, *About Shy Boy,* www.montyroberts.com/ab_about_shyboy.html.

2. Monty Roberts, *Shy Boy* (New York: Perennial, 1999), 27.

3. Ibid., 234, 236.

4. Shy Boy's story was compiled based on information taken from the book *Shy Boy* by Monty Roberts (Perennial, 1999).

CHAPTER 23: *Living in the Lion's Den*

1. William Carr Peel, *Living in the Lions' Den without Being Eaten* (Colorado Springs: NavPress, 1994), 212.

2. *John Wesley: Holiness of Heart and Life, A Spiritual Resource Guide;* www.gbgm-umc.org/umw/wesley/wilber.stm#2.

3. William Wilberforce's story was compiled based on information from www.brycchancarey.com/abolition/wilberforce.htm and http://en.wikipedia.org/wiki/William_Wilberforce.

4. Dr. Myles Munroe, "The wealthiest place on earth." Text supplied to the author by Dr. Munroe at the Columbus Leadership Prayer Breakfast, October 30, 2002.

5. Philip Yancey, *Reaching for the Invisible God* (Grand Rapids: Zondervan, 2000), 42.

CHAPTER 24: *Claiming Your Authority*

1. The headline and text of the newspaper article is based on the author's memory of an October 1983 article in *The Columbus Dispatch.*

2. Pope John Paul II, in his first address in St. Peter's Square after being elected pope, October 22, 1978.

3. Anthony T. Evans, *America's Only Hope* (Chicago: Moody, 1990), 65.

4. Jim Wallis, *God's Politics* (San Francisco: Harper, 2005), 4.

CHAPTER 26: *The Kingdom of God*

1. Stanley Weintraub, *Silent Night: The Story of The World War I Christmas Truce* (New York: Penguin, 2001), xvi.

2. Ibid., 5.

ABOUT THE AUTHOR

Harvey Hook is the founder and executive director of The Gathering/Columbus, an organization that addresses the moral, ethical, and spiritual needs of business, professional, and government leaders. The Gathering partners with individuals, churches, and other organizations for the purpose of connecting men and women with a small-group experience designed to meet their personal, spiritual, and social needs.

Harvey launched the Columbus chapter of The Gathering in 1998, following eleven years of work with incarcerated and at-risk inner-city teens (with YFC/Youth Guidance, USA), and six years of work with severely and profoundly retarded adults and children.

Harvey is a graduate of the State University of New York (Albany), with a bachelor's degree in psychology, and Denver Seminary, with a master's degree in counseling.

He hosts a weekly television interview program, called *The Gathering,* which airs nationally on the Sky Angel satellite network.

Harvey and Rita Hook have been married for twenty-five years. They live in Dublin, Ohio, and have two daughters, Rebecca and Rachel.

The Columbus branch of The Gathering is affiliated with The Gathering/USA, an international organization headquartered in Orlando, Florida.

Programs of The Gathering include The Leadership Forum, which provides leadership and character-development training to address such critical areas as personal and corporate values, ethics, and integrity; and The Youth Initiative Project, a partnership of local and national businesses that serve the moral, educational, and character-development needs of youth.

Each year, The Gathering/Columbus sponsors a number of breakfasts where a local or national leader has the platform to share his or her faith with other business, professional, and government leaders. These include the Ohio Prayer Breakfast, in conjuction with the National Day of Prayer, and a fall Leadership Prayer Breakfast.

The Gathering/Columbus also partners with Mission Emanuel, an outreach ministry of The Gathering/USA that brings together people from around the world dedicated to improving the lives of people in the Dominican Republic by providing health care, education, and better living conditions. Teams from The Gathering travel to the Dominican Republic four to six times per year for the purpose of renovating, expanding, and building medical, dental, and school facilities to meet the needs of some of the poorest citizens in our hemisphere. ✓

CONTACT THE AUTHOR

For more information about Harvey Hook and the mission and work of The Gathering, visit the following Web sites:

www.HarveyHook.com

www.ThePowerOfAnOrdinaryLife.com

www.GatheringColumbus.com